# I Never Promised

# You a Cookbook

Also by Rita Papazian

*Remembering Fairfield Connecticut: Famous People & Historic Places*

*Gioacchino: Memoir of an Italian Immigrant*

# I Never Promised

# You a Cookbook

Rita Papazian

The essay "Aprons and Their Gesture of Love" first appeared in *Around the Table: Food Memoirs from Fairfield,* published by the Fairfield Public Library in 2011.

ISBN-13: 978-1720690450

ISBN-10: 1720690456

*For*
*Gabriel, Alexandra, Cameron, Zachary,*
*Calum and Vivienne*
*with love*

# Contents

# About This Cookbook

With a nod to Carl Sandburg and his poem "The Fog," my decision to write this cookbook came to me "on little cat feet." Slowly and quietly, I began to think about taking on this project as I sat in my apartment at my computer looking straight ahead through the sliding glass doors in my living room, out onto the balcony and to the trees beyond. It is a pretty setting that lends itself to opening the mind, and yes, I would say, the spirit that has moved me forward.

And so, I began with the thought that this book would be a combination of memoir and cookbook with the basis, of course, food. As you, the reader, will see, the memoir part consists of a few personal essays with a focus on family and food coupled with articles I wrote about celebrity chefs, who had written cookbooks and were publicizing them at bookstores in Connecticut. I reported on these book-signings for a local newspaper.

I like the idea of writing a memoir cookbook, for the concept brings a personal and professional dimension to the cookbook project. Compiling family recipes into a book can spur memories often tucked away. The mundane task of copying these recipes into book form unleashes memories and brings an added dimension to the food preparation, cooking and consumption.

The recipes come mainly from my mother's recipe file and my own. These include many of the recipes that either I or my mother made mostly the last 30 years or so of the twentieth century, before this country really turned its focus on so-called "gourmet" dishes and those that reflected the latest trend in eating and diets. There is nothing terribly unusual about these recipes, but they do represent my family with its Italian influences and when I was married, the Armenian influences as well. Generally, these recipes are easy to make and not very time-consuming; yet, offer a variety.

I have written this book for my family and friends and for the extended family of food lovers, in hopes that others may find the joy in compiling their own recipes into a cookbook, and better yet, a memoir cookbook. I never promised a cookbook. Surprise! Here it is.

# Introduction

Cooking brings me a comfort and a sense of security. The process is calming for me, and if it is a recipe that I recall having as a child, it brings me back to that time and place. When people like celebrity chefs and cookbook authors talk about family recipes, they inevitably talk about how they learned to cook from their mothers and grandmothers. Often, it is the grandmother.

Unfortunately, I cannot say I learned how to cook from my grandmothers or even my mother. My two grandmothers died before I was born. I had two grandfathers and knew only one of them. My maternal grandfather lived in a multi-family house in the Bronx. He was a music teacher who taught every instrument. The students would come to his second floor apartment, which included a small room with an upright piano along one wall. Here is where he conducted his lessons. His second wife, Grandma Martha, would leave in the morning to go to her job at the telephone company in New York City. Grandpa was the house-husband. He stayed home, taught his music lessons and cooked dinner.

My mother and I would visit my grandfather. I recall the cooking aromas that would permeate the apartment, especially fried dishes. The one take-away image I have is that my grandfather would dry hot peppers in a pantry in the kitchen. I would walk into the kitchen and pass the pantry where I would see hot peppers hanging on strings. Once they were dried and wrinkled, my grandfather would cut the string and fry the peppers in hot olive oil. As they fried, the peppers would crackle and pop up. Then, we would sit at the kitchen table covered in an oil cloth. My grandfather would bring over a plate of fried hot peppers, and my mother and I would begin to torture ourselves. The taste was delicious, but the peppers were so hot — in taste, not temperature — that we would stuff our mouths with Italian bread that was at the ready. Eating bread along with the peppers was the only way to survive this Italian custom. That was the extent of my cooking lesson with a grandparent.

People assume that I must have grown up learning to cook standing next to my mother in our small kitchen in our split-level house on Long Island in the 1950s. Wrong! I don't recall my mother teaching me how to cook. She cooked in the kitchen, and I inhaled the aromas. I observed the signs of tomato sauce with meatballs and braciole cooking atop the stove on Sunday morning — even some Thursday evenings. That's what Italians do. Cook sauce on Sundays. It is a tradition that I still love to hold onto, even if it is just to serve myself a plate of pasta on a Sunday evening. Growing up, I would watch my mother serve the pasta dinner on Sunday afternoon, usually around 3 p.m., especially if we had company. We had a lot of company growing up. Aunts, uncles and cousins would visit each other's houses, usually on a Sunday; my parents' friends would visit; or we would visit their houses.

I observed how and what my mother cooked. I noticed that my mother would serve a balanced meal. The dinner menu consisted mainly of a meat or fish served with salad, a starch (noodles, rice or potatoes) and a vegetable. Of course, often there was what Italians like to call "a first dish," which would be a soup or, if it's Sunday, a pasta. Weekends or holidays a first dish could be more elaborate, such as an antipasto (before the pasta).

I carried my observations of my mother's cooking into every kitchen that would be part of my home. Along the way, I observed the meals, especially those my Aunt Margaret or my Aunt Mary would serve. Aunt Margaret was one of my father's four sisters. He was the youngest of eight children, four of whom were born in Italy. Therefore, the older the relatives were the more they cooked traditional Italian dishes. My Aunt Mary was my mother's sister-in-law. She was married to my mother's brother David and both their children, David and Christine, spent many years working in the food industry. So, I did a lot of observing, eating and asking questions. To this day, I like to call up my cousin David in Florida and ask him how he makes something.

Today, I live near two of my six grandchildren, Vivienne and Calum, and I enjoy having them to my house for dinner. I like to give them a little cooking lesson so they can begin their own tradition of cooking with their "grandmother," something I never had the pleasure of doing. I also like to visit my grandchildren Zachary and Cameron in Massachusetts and do some cooking there. What is interesting is that during one of my visits, it was

Zachary who taught me how to make an apple pie. That was quite a moment for me because baking is not really my strong suit. Zachary is very good at baking. He and his brother, Cameron, enjoy baking with their mom. I also enjoy my other grandchildren, Gabriel and Alexandra, who also live in Massachusetts. They can teach me more than I can teach them. They cook with their father, my son, Norman, who enjoys cooking. Whenever I ask Norman how he learned to make a dish, he responds, "On the Internet." Times have certainly changed.

Norman may learn to cook something by getting the recipe from the Internet, but I am proud to say that what he cooks and serves, especially for holidays, continues the family's traditions. For example, when he hosts the family for a holiday dinner, you can bet on Norman making a lamb roast, a tradition that comes from his paternal grandmother, Yepress, an Armenian who emigrated from Turkey, who would serve us either a lamb roast or a roast beef when my children were young. I would continue her tradition in planning my own holiday meals and also for barbecuing shish-kebob, a summer dinner the family would enjoy.

One would expect that my mother-in-law's shish-kebob must be from a special recipe because it tasted so good. Not really. Yes, she would marinate the lamb overnight. However, the lamb kebobs, well-salted and peppered, would marinate only in chopped onions. The salt, pepper and onions would do magic with the lamb, especially when grilled on an outdoor grill. The meat would be grilled with green peppers, onions and mushrooms and then served with pilaf and stuffed grape leaves.

Lamb kebobs and pasta, among other dishes, are now part of my family's cuisine and, as one celebrity chef said, "part of the American quilt, a patchwork of recipes brought to this country that have become modified in their adaptation to the American way of life."

# Aprons and Their Gesture of Love

Growing up, I never saw my mother wearing an apron at the dinner table. Years later, when my husband and I would visit his mother in Queens, New York, I never saw my mother-in-law with her apron off. Different households, different cultures.

In my mother's Italian-American culture, the apron came off when it was time to sit down to eat. The gesture was of the tradition of looking one's best. And sure enough, the dinner table was the setting for proper attire and good behavior.

On the other hand, my Armenian mother-in-law, Yepress, believed the apron stayed on, a sign she was there to serve others throughout dinner. She would shuttle between the kitchen and the dining room. She would increase her pacing with each new grandchild at the table. I don't know if she ever really ate a complete meal herself. She would pick at the food during her cooking and make herself a plate after everyone else had almost finished eating. After each step in the cooking, serving and cleaning up, she would wipe her hands on the apron tied around her waist.

Yepress usually wore a thin nondescript apron, faded from years of cooking in the cramped back kitchen of a two-story, semi-detached brick house among rows of similar houses separated by a shared driveway in Bayside, Queens, New York. It seemed she always wore the same apron, whether serving her family or spending hours preparing the rice and onion mixture that she stuffed into grape leaves. One day she taught me how to stuff the grape leaves, an Armenian specialty.

Days earlier, Yepress had picked the grape leaves from vines familiar to her in the neighborhood. Then, she would steam them in a pot while she cooked the mixture of onions and rice. Once the ingredients were ready for assembly, she demonstrated the proper way to take each leaf, drop a tablespoon of the onion-and-rice mixture onto it and then fold the leaf in such a way to avoid any mixture spilling out. Making stuffed grape leaves was even more tedious than making the lasagna my mother had taught me to make growing up.

My mother, whose aprons were more colorful and decorative than my mother-in-law's apron, would often wear aprons that she had sewn herself on the sewing machine in the small room on the second floor of our Dutch Colonial house in Yonkers, New York, where I had spent my childhood. There she would take remnants of fabric from the dresses she had sewn for me to wear to P.S.21 in the late 1940s. My mother loved the domestic arts. She knew her role in the nuclear family, and she never expressed discontentment, or, if she were unhappy, she certainly kept it to herself. She channeled her energies into sewing, cooking and gardening, and guided her children's development with a motherly instinct, not psychology books.

The aprons of my mother's and mother-in-law's generation represented a badge of honor for these women, and in essence, defined their role in the household. They were there to feed and serve the family.

Through the years, I have taken my apron out of the kitchen. I donned my full blue apron for work purposes. The apron had a string that went around the neck and one that tied around the waist. It had a pocket in the front in which I would keep a special pen that I would use to mark up pages during production of the weekly newspaper I edited for many years. It was a handy little pocket and apron, and I felt a sense of pride to have reached the position of community newspaper editor.

However, that role is gone now. As I continue to do freelance work, I have also returned more to the kitchen. I find pleasure in the domestic arts as my mother had. Recently, as the holidays approached, my daughter asked me whether I wanted a coffee mug, mouse pad, puzzle, ornament, tee-shirt or an apron. I had gathered it was something one of her children was making in pre-school to give as a gift. I chose an apron.

I was right. On Christmas Day in 2010, five-year-old Zachary presented me with a white apron, similar in style to the one I had worn as an editor in production. Instead of the pocket, there was a large colorful rainbow with semi-circular brushstrokes of orange, blue, green, purple and red at the bodice.

The apron underscores this stage in my life in which I receive equal pleasure in the creative and culinary arts. Yet, it is a reminder of that one role—the maternal role—we, women, are given in life that continues to hold significance as we gather around the family table, whether the apron is on or off.

# Taking Pride in Pyrex's Stirring of Memories

I have a set of Pyrex nested mixing bowls, each a different color: blue, red, green and yellow. My daughter Ellen gave them to me many years ago as a birthday gift. She remembered how I had talked about getting a set similar to the one that my mother had cooked with when I was growing up. There is something very comforting about cooking in the kitchen with the equipment I recall in childhood.

In addition to the mixing bowls, I also have a cone-shaped colander, a hand-held juicer, and a manual grinder—all quite ancient when you consider what you now can buy in William Sonoma, Crate and Barrel, or, of course, Macy's.

However, it is the set of mixing bowls that quite attracts me. I keep them on my kitchen counter, despite the fact that I have very little counter space in my one-bedroom apartment. Maybe, it is because they were so frequently used in the kitchen of my childhood that the image of them has stayed with me all these years. Also, it seems that each particular size served a purpose and still does today as I reach for them to prepare a meal or set out the ingredients to do some baking.

The smallest is a five-and-three-quarter-inch blue bowl, handy for scrambling an egg, for you can easily tilt the bowl slightly as you whip the egg with a fork. The next one is a seven-inch red bowl, just right for preparing a mixture of breadcrumbs, grated cheese and parsley with seasonings, moistened with olive oil and red wine vinegar to stuff Cubanelle peppers, those long Italian light-green peppers that my mother would prepare. The next to the largest bowl is an eight-and-a-half-inch green bowl, practical for a variety of food preparations, such as washing salad, draining noodles or creaming butter and sugar during the baking of cookies. This green bowl size is also practical, in itself, to serve the salad. The largest bowl is a ten-and-a-half-inch yellow bowl, a mammoth size in the kitchen and useful when making cakes and cookies when the recipe calls for one to do all that sifting of flour and baking powder separate from the creaming process. This bright yellow bowl is also a colorful serving piece filled with macaroni or potato salad to place on picnic tables for summer barbecues.

These mixing bowls that now sit out on my kitchen counter are a constant reminder of my childhood and my mother cooking in the kitchen. Of course, I am protective of them and ask visitors in the kitchen not to use them. Instead, I offer a more durable stainless steel bowl that I keep inside the cabinets.

In addition to the mixing bowls, I have a vintage metal strainer/colander that you place on a stand. It comes with a wooden pestle, a useful tool for straining. I like to use this colander mainly for two purposes: to strain tomatoes for homemade tomato sauce or to strain cooked apples for making applesauce (straining eliminates the seeds and skins from both). Of course, I am sure there is modern kitchen equipment that can accomplish the same purpose. But, I like the churning, the repetitive circulative movement of my arm and hand that pushes the substantive parts of the tomato and apple through the tiny holes.

The third vintage piece of kitchen equipment is the juicer, a Wear-Ever aluminum citrus contraption that you open up to put in your half-orange or lemon and grasp the two handles tightly to extract the juice. This is not an easy process, but when I see the juice coming out, I feel a sense of accomplishment.

The meat grinder is the fourth piece of kitchen equipment that comes from my mother's kitchen. While I hardly use this grinder any more, when I did, I used it to grind cranberries for making fresh cranberry-orange relish. I put the cranberries into the grinder and use the hand crank to chop up the cranberries. Again, this is a satisfying endeavor.

# Antipasto, Appetizers and Dips

## Antipasto

Antipasto is an assortment of foods served before the main meal. Celebrity chef Lidia Matticchio Bastianich refers to antipasto as "little bites to nibble." These foods include smoked or pickled meats, cheeses, vegetables, olives, etc. When I was growing up, my mother would serve one platter, offering a variety of meat, vegetables and cheeses all mixed together. The amounts and selection of ingredients depend upon taste:

**Anchovies**

**Artichoke, marinated (bought in a jar)**

**Capers**

**Celery, chopped**

**Cheese, provolone, sliced or cubed**

**Olives, black or green**

**Peppers, fried ( bought in a jar)**

**Peppers, roasted red (pimento) (bought in a jar) cut into small pieces and sprinkled with oregano**

**Salami, Genoa or Soppressata, slices or cubed**

**Seasonings: olive oil, balsamic vinegar, garlic powder, salt and pepper**

After mixing all the ingredients together, sprinkle the antipasto with garlic powder, salt, pepper, olive oil and balsamic vinegar. Chill before serving.

Instead of this one big dish of antipasto, for variety, at times, I will serve an antipasto assortment of foods, meats, cheeses, vegetables, seafood and olives presented individually on one platter. Or, I like to serve this popular choice: tomato and mozzarella slices layered alternately on a platter and drizzled with olive oil.

**Anchovy Twists**

**8 ounces soft cream cheese**

**1 cup soft butter**

**2 ¼ cups flour**

**4 two-ounce cans anchovy fillets**

**1 egg, lightly beaten**

Preheat oven to 375 degrees.

Beat the cream cheese and butter together. Stir in the flour and mix well. Wrap the dough in wax paper and chill at least four hours or overnight.

Divide the dough into quarters. Roll out one-quarter on a lightly floured board to a rectangle about 12" by 6."

Pat the excess oil from one can of anchovy fillets and line up the fillets in rows, one-half inch apart, over half the dough. Moisten dough between fillets with water. Fold over other half of the dough and press down in between the fillets.

Cut into sticks so that each one encloses an anchovy. Twist slightly and place on a baking sheet. Brush with the egg and bake 15 minutes or until lightly brown and done. Repeat with the remaining dough and anchovies. Yields about 48 anchovy twists.

Note: These will keep in a tightly-covered tin for two weeks.

## Artichoke Cheese Dip

½ cup mayonnaise

½ cup shredded cheddar cheese

½ cup shredded Monterey Jack cheese

⅛ teaspoon onion salt

⅛ teaspoon lemon pepper

½ (14 ounce) can artichoke hearts, drained

Preheat oven 350 degrees.

Combine all ingredients. Mix well and pour into a two-quart baking dish. Bake uncovered for 30 minutes. Serve with toasted French bread, tortilla chips or garlic bread.

## Cheese Balls

¾ cup margarine or butter

5 ounces grated cheddar cheese

1 ½ cups flour

½ tablespoon salt

Preheat oven 350 degrees.

Cream together the above ingredients. Roll into small balls and bake on ungreased cookie sheet (allow space for spreading) for 30 to 35 minutes.

## Crab Delight Dip

Combine and chill:

**1 cup mayonnaise**

**1 tablespoon sherry**

**2 6.5 ounce cans of crabmeat, drained**

**½ cup sour cream**

**1 teaspoon lemon juice**

**Salt and pepper**

## Dipping Sauce for Raw Vegetables

Blend in blender and then chill until serving:

**18 anchovies**

**1 lemon peeled**

**3 cloves garlic**

**1 teaspoon pepper**

**1 cup olive oil**

**½ cup parsley**

## Eggplant Spread

**2 medium or 1 large eggplant**

**2 large garlic cloves, finely chopped**

**2 tablespoons fresh parsley, chopped**

**2 tablespoons lemon juice**

**1 tablespoon olive oil**

**Ground pepper to taste**

Preheat oven to 350 degrees

Prick eggplant in several places with a fork. Place on a baking sheet and cook in oven for one hour. Let eggplant cool. Cut eggplant in half and with a spoon, scrape out the flesh into a bowl, discarding the skin. With a fork, mash together eggplant, garlic, parsley, lemon juice, olive oil and pepper. Cover and refrigerate. Serve as an appetizer with crusty bread or pita, or as a dip for fresh vegetables.

**Note:**

My mother-in-law, Yepress Papazian, would scoop out the eggplant and then add chopped raw onion and parsley, and serve as a vegetable dish.

**Fruit Dip**

Mix pineapple, strawberries, sour cream, honey and a bit of cinnamon. Chill.

**Jarlsberg Puffs**

**1 cup water**

**¼ cup (½ stick) butter or margarine**

**¾ cup unsifted all-purpose flour**

**4 eggs**

**1 ½ cups shredded Jarlsberg cheese**

**Dash cayenne pepper**

**Hot oil**

In a saucepan, bring water and butter to a full boil. Add flour all at once and beat well until mixture forms into a ball and pulls away from sides of pan. Remove from heat.

Add eggs, one at a time, and beat until well blended. Blend in cheese and cayenne pepper. Drop by spoonful into hot oil and cook until golden brown on both sides. Turn only once. Drain on absorbent paper. Makes about 30 puffs.

**Olives in Pie Crust**

**1 package pie crust**

**1 cup shredded cheddar cheese**

**¼ teaspoon dry mustard**

**2 teaspoons paprika**

**Green olives**

Preheat oven to 425 degrees

Prepare pie crust as directed. Thoroughly mix in cheese, paprika and dry mustard. Put one teaspoon pie crust mixture around each olive. Freeze or can be baked immediately for 10 to 12 minutes.

**Onion Sticks**

**12 slices white bread**

**1 envelope Lipton onion soup mix**

**½ pound butter**

Preheat oven to 375 degrees

Trim crusts from bread and toast bread. Cut each slice into five strips. Spread dry onion soup on waxed paper. Dip toast strips in melted butter; then roll in dry soup coating both sides well. Bake 9 to 10 minutes or until golden.


**Sauerkraut Balls**

**1 onion minced**

**¼ cup butter**

**1 ⅓ cups ground ham**

**½ cup flour**

**¼ cup sauerkraut juice**

**1 14 ounce can sauerkraut, drained (save juice) and chopped**

**1 egg beaten**

**¼ cup milk**

**Breadcrumbs**

Cook onion in butter until soft. Stir in ham and 1/4 cup flour. Add broth and sauerkraut. Cook, stirring constantly for five minutes. Cool. Form into small balls with one teaspoon of mixture. Roll in flour. Dip in combined egg and milk. Roll in breadcrumbs. Fry in vegetable oil until brown.

## Spinach Dip

**1 package frozen chopped spinach, thawed and drained well**

**½ cup chopped fresh parsley**

**3 tablespoons chopped green scallions, including green tops**

**½ teaspoon salt**

**½ teaspoon pepper**

**⅔ cup mayonnaise**

**2 tablespoons sour cream.**

Mix all ingredients and refrigerate overnight.

## Swedish Meatballs

**1 pound chop meat**

**2 slices stale white bread**

**1 egg**

**Milk sufficient to soak bread**

**Flour sufficient to flour meatballs**

**#2 can crushed tomatoes**

**2 onions**

**1 teaspoon Worcestershire sauce**

**Salt and pepper**

Soak bread until soft. Beat egg. Mix egg, bread and chop meat. Add salt and pepper. Shape into balls. Roll in flour and fry. Put balls in slightly greased pot over low heat. Pour water into fry pan and then put into pot covering balls. Cut onions and add to pot. Add tomatoes and Worcestershire sauce. Simmer two hours.

**Swiss Fondue**

**2 cups grated natural Swiss cheese (1/2 pound)**

**1 ½ teaspoons flour**

**1 clove garlic, optional**

**¾ cup Sauterne wine**

**¼ teaspoon salt**

**1 ½ teaspoon Tabasco sauce**

**⅛ teaspoon nutmeg**

**French bread, cut into bite-sized cubes**

Toss grated cheese with flour. Rub skillet or blazer of chafing dish with garlic. Pour in wine. Cook over low heat until almost boiling. Add cheese. Stir until melted. Add salt, Tabasco and nutmeg.

To serve, spear bread cubes with fork or toothpick. Dunk. If fondue becomes too thick, add more wine. Yields 3 to 4 main dish servings or 6 to 8 appetizer servings.

# Michel Nischan's Recipes Connect Food, Family and Health

Chef Michel Nischan, cookbook writer and culinary advocate, wants to clear a health-conscious path to food lovers' hearts as well as their appetites.

This father of five has been spreading the importance of cooking and eating healthy meals in talks, food demonstrations, television documentaries, and school events, as well as through his many cookbooks. These are: "Taste Pure and Simple: Recipes for Good Food and Good Health," "Sustainably Delicious" and "Homegrown Pure and Simple," based upon his family's gardening and recipes.

During an interview Nischan discussed his philosophy about eating healthy. "Nature has all the answers for us without having to come up with the sophisticated manufacturing processes that create these foods of convenience," Nischan says, "Leave things as close to nature as possible. If we're careful about the ingredients we choose and inventive in some of our cooking techniques, we don't need a lot of processed foods we eat that are the pillar of a lot of our cooking.

"We don't need reduced heavy cream to make a great sauce; we don't need eggs to bind the salad dressing; we don't need flour to thicken pan gravy," he says. "We can juice a Yukon potato and put into the pan juices from the roasted turkey and have beautiful pan gravy using natural starch.

"We can reduce beet juice and pour it over ice cream. Reduced beet juice with a split vanilla bean poured over ice cream is a sensational thing."

In regards to cooking healthfully when the holidays come around, Nischan says, "You want to have an abundant holiday as anyone can have, but you want to do it in a way that is healthful." Through the years, he has tried to cook foods during the holiday that are overtly indulgent but do not have such of an impact on a person's health.

"We just need to think outside the box a little bit," Nischan said. He has ideas for buying, cooking and eating quality foods that place responsibility not only on the consumer but also the community and government as well.

First, he begins in the home where Nischan gardens with his family. He encourages families to garden and cook together in the kitchen. "It is so much more intimate and so much more culturally connected," he says. "It's not important that one of my kids becomes one of the top singers in the choir at school or one of the top soccer players on the local team. That's not cultural connection; that's competition. When I can work in the kitchen with my children, they learn how to cook more; they learn how to appreciate food more. We're cooking fresher food; we're spending face time together doing something really together.

"When they are involved in the cooking process, they may be more interested in tasting something they never had tried before," he says. "It's wrong for parents to want to take their kids to all these activities at the expense of the food that they eat. There's nothing that connects us more closely to our real culture than the way we prepare and share our food. That's what really makes a statement about who we are as a people and where we live."

Encouraging families to garden and cook together are activities stemming from Nischan's childhood growing up in Des Plaines, Ill., not on a farm but in a suburban home set on a quarter acre of land.

"My mom, basically said, 'We don't need a yard; we need to eat well.' She dug up the whole backyard. She also sent us to my grandfather's family in Missouri for a month in the summer to learn how to treat animals, how to do chores, how to respect the land.

"I'm the product of a really amazing mother. She saw that food was the most intimate connection we have left with the earth. The way we treat the land, the way we treat animals, the way we cook it, the way we eat, the grace with which we serve—the genuine intent determines who we are and what we are about."

# Salads

## Ambrosia

Mix and chill the following ingredients:

**2 cups pineapple chunks**

**1 cup mandarin oranges**

**½ package miniature marshmallows**

**½ package shredded coconut**

**1 ½ pint sour cream**

**Maraschino cherries halved for garnish.**


## Classic Waldorf Salad

**½ cup mayonnaise**

**1 tablespoon sugar**

**1 tablespoon lemon juice**

**½ teaspoon salt**

**3 medium apples, diced**

**1 cup sliced celery**

**½ cup- chopped walnuts**

Combine first four ingredients. Stir in remaining ingredients. Cover. Chill. Makes five and one-half cups.

## Cole Slaw

1 large head of cabbage

2 medium onions

¾ cup sugar

Chop cabbage and onions. Add sugar and mix

Boil:

¾ cup white vinegar

¾ cup salad oil

1 tbs. salt

2 tsp. sugar

1 tsp. dry mustard

1 tsp. celery seed

Immediately pour mixture over the chopped cabbage and onions. Refrigerate. (This cole slaw will keep for at least a week. The longer it set, the better it tastes.)

## Creamy Italian Pasta Salad

1 cup mayonnaise

2 tablespoons red wine vinegar

1 clove minced garlic

1 teaspoon dried basil

1 teaspoon salt

**1 ¼ teaspoon pepper**

**1 pound Fusilli macaroni**

**1 cup quartered cherry tomatoes**

**½ cup chopped green pepper**

**½ cup sliced olives**

Combine first six ingredients. Cook macaroni and strain. Add tomatoes, green pepper and olives. Mix in mayonnaise mixture. Chill.

**Cucumber Salad**

**1 package lime Jell-O**

**¼ teaspoon salt**

**¾ cup boiling water**

**1 tablespoon lemon juice**

**1 ¼ cups cold water**

**1 cup chopped cucumber, seeded**

**1 tablespoon minced onion'**

**1 teaspoon dill weed**

**½ cup sour cream**

Mix lime Jell-O with salt and boiling water Add lemon juice and cold water. Add cucumber, onion and dill. Place in refrigerator until Jell-O firms. Serve with a sour cream on top.

## Macaroni Salad

1 cup mayonnaise

2 tablespoons vinegar

1 tablespoon mustard

1 teaspoon sugar

1 teaspoon salt

¼ teaspoon pepper

8 ounces elbow macaroni (cooked)

1 cup celery

1 cup chopped green or red pepper

¼ cup chopped onion

Combine first six ingredients. Stir in remaining ingredients. Cover Chill. Makes five cups

## Onion and Orange Salad

4 oranges

1 red onion

½ teaspoon crushed rosemary

6 tablespoons olive oil

1 ½ tablespoons vinegar

2 tablespoons orange juice

**Salt and pepper**

**Romaine or Chicory greens**

Peel and slice oranges. Slice onion and break into rings. Combine orange and onion with rosemary. Mix oil, vinegar, juice, salt and pepper. Add to oranges. Just before serving add Romaine or Chicory greens.

Here's another idea for oranges:

Peel an orange and slice thin. Dust with confectioner's sugar. Sprinkle with cinnamon.

**Hot Potato Salad**

**2 ½ pounds potatoes**

**3 tablespoons red wine vinegar**

**6 tablespoons olive oil**

**Salt and pepper**

**⅓ cup onion**

**2 tablespoons chopped parsley**

Boil potatoes in salted water. Cut in halves or quarters. Toss with vinegar, oil, onion and parsley. Salt and pepper to taste.

## Potato Salad

1 cup mayonnaise

2 tablespoons vinegar

1 ½ teaspoon salt

1 teaspoon sugar

¼ teaspoon pepper

4 cups cooked, peeled and cubed potatoes (5 to 6 medium potatoes)

1 cup celery sliced

½ cup chopped onion

2 hard cooked eggs, chopped.

Combine first five ingredients and add to potatoes. Stir in remaining ingredients. Cover. Makes five cups.

## Nana Mallett's Salad Recipes

My mother's recipe file included six salad recipes, five of which just list ingredients, no measurements. I can picture her having lunch with friends either in their homes or at a function at the senior center where she would delight in the served salad and make note or ask about the ingredients. These recipes appear to have been written quickly, either in a red, green or black pen. I would guess that maybe she carried index cards in her purse or at least a small memo notebook and would jot down the ingredients.

Here are the salad recipes. The first lists the full ingredients and method.

### Bean Salad

**1 can green beans**

**1 can marrow beans**

**1 can kidney beans**

**½ cup chopped onions**

**½ cup green pepper**

**⅔ cup vinegar**

**⅓ cup salad oil**

**¼ cup sugar**

**1 teaspoon salt**

**¼ teaspoon pepper**

Drain and combine cans of beans. Add peppers and onions. Combine sugar, vinegar, salad oil, salt and pepper. Pour over beans. Chill. Toss before serving.

## Caesar Salad

Romaine Lettuce, Lemon Juice, Salt, Garlic Powder, Anchovies, Parmesan Cheese, Croutons, Salad Oil.

## Tossed Salad

Boston Lettuce and Cherry Tomatoes

## Chef's Salad

Ham, Cheese, Turkey, Green Pepper, Tomatoes, Lettuce

## Chicken Salad

Boiled Chicken Cut-Up in Small Chunk-Sized Pieces. Celery, Apple, Grapes, Walnuts, Capers, Mayonnaise

## Escarole and Raw Mushrooms

Mushrooms, Escarole, Slivered Pimentos, Anchovies, Salt and Pepper, Italian Dressing

# Food Carts Sell More Than Hot Dogs Nowadays

For years, I have wanted to man one of those hot dog carts. I have no idea how or why this idea came to me. But it seems whenever the warm weather pops up, so do the hot dog carts, and I'm jealous. I say to myself, "How did that person do it? How did that person get that enviable spot?" I notice that at some big box stores there is usually a hot dog cart on the property. How did they get to do that?

I thought what a great job to have. You can make money doling out hot dogs and during the downtime read a book. Pretty easy stuff, no doubt.

Mobile food carts and food trucks are certainly the trend these days. It's amazing how creative people can be. They've become creative not only in the type of food offerings, but also in the design of the cart or mobile unit itself.

A few years ago while visiting family in Naples, Fla., I took a photograph of a lemonade stand. This was not your typical lemonade stand. The cart itself, which looked as if it had been a two-wheel flower pushcart, had a large lemon constructed atop of the two wheels. An ice cooler straddled the cart's two handles and on top of that the vendor had placed a large thermos from which he dispensed the lemonade. The vendor sat beneath a large yellow-and-white umbrella to escape from the unmerciful hot Florida summer sun that was beating down on him.

I thought of that lemonade stand recently when in a Connecticut town, I saw a meatball food cart towed by a tiny Smart Car. The vendor cooked his hamburgers on a grill on the cart. Another vendor that has attracted pedestrian traffic is a vendor who sells crepes from his yellow bread-truck style vehicle that he parks on a main street near a library. He hooks his equipment to a generator that he places on the sidewalk, and when it's running it can be heard inside the nearby library. Of course, this is not conducive to reading inside a quiet library.

One time I wrote a feature article about a sandwich food truck that parked near a beach in a shoreline town. The idea of a food truck again fascinated me. I climbed aboard and stood inside near the window watching as the young couple waited on customers and cooked the food on the grill. They featured a lot of wrap sandwiches. It reminded me of the many times my friend and I would travel around the country in an RV. We would sightsee at many national and state parks and then eat and sleep in the camper parked in a campsite. There is something comforting about small enclosed spaces.

When you drive up I-95, you can see how popular these food trucks have become as you peer out your window in the Long Wharf area in New Haven, Connecticut, where the food trucks are parked along the shoreline. They have become very popular and have increased in numbers in recent years in that area. I can see the popularity of that location for food trucks because there is not much around that shore area, which is a popular spot to enjoy.

I went to a one-day outdoor market one time in a Fairfield County town. The market sold lots of arts and crafts, clothing, cookies, Italian products, garden accessories and art work. The market was complemented with two food trucks selling the typical fast-food, as well as that hamburger cart guy. Cute, yes, but I felt a little sorry for the restaurants just a few doors from where the market was set up. Here, this market had attracted a lot of people from out of town, no doubt, and here it would have been a good opportunity to attract those visitors into the local restaurants for a hamburger or pizza.

These food carts and food trucks certainly represent a lot of ingenuity and enterprise, but local officials should keep in mind the storekeepers who are paying rent to keep our downtowns viable. It's great to have food vendors in areas where there is no opportunity to buy something to eat. I especially praise the creativity that is creeping into the traditional food cart and truck. Just walk around Manhattan streets and see the variety. We really have come full circle in the city where food carts sell a wide variety of foods, including the basic fruit—apples, oranges, bananas, just like the old days.

# Soups

## Avgolemono Soup

**8 cups chicken broth**

**½ cup washed rice**

**Salt**

**2 whole eggs**

**2 egg yolks**

**Juice of 2 lemons**

Bring broth to boil. Add rice and cook until tender. Salt to taste. Beat the eggs and egg yolks together until light and frothy. Slowly beat in the lemon juice. Add a little of the hot broth to the egg-lemon mixture, blending it well so that the eggs do not curdle. Slowly add to the broth in the pan, stirring constantly. Heat through. Do not allow to boil.

## The Famous United States Senate Restaurant Bean Soup

**2 pounds navy beans**

**1 ½ pounds smoked ham hocks**

**1 onion, chopped**

**2 tablespoons butter**

**Salt and pepper to taste**

Wash beans and run through hot water until beans are white again. Put on the fire with four quarts of hot water. Then add the ham hocks and slowly boil the ham hocks and beans for approximately three hours in covered pot. Braise one onion chopped in a little butter and when light brown put in bean soup. Season with salt and pepper when ready to serve.


## Beef and Vegetable Soup

The amount of each ingredient in this recipe depends upon the number of servings. When I make soup, I like to have enough for two or three meals, for example, two dinners and a lunch for one or two people. Therefore, I list the ingredients accordingly.

**2 pounds beef bones for stock**

**2 pounds beef shank and/or beef short ribs**

**Olive oil**

**Tomato paste**

**¼ cup apple cider vinegar**

**3 carrots, peeled and coarsely chopped**

**3 celery stalks, coarsely chopped**

**2 onions, peeled and quartered**

**1 (14.5-ounce) can tomatoes, whole (with liquid) or four fresh tomatoes quartered**

**String beans, optional**

**Chickpeas, optional**

**Parsley, one-half bunch**

**Thyme, one-half bunch**

**Salt and pepper to taste**

**Pasta, such as Ditalli or Tubetti**

Preheat oven to 350 degrees

Place meat and bones in a roasting pan. Coat with olive oil and tomato paste. Roast until browned, approximately one-half hour. Transfer bones and meat to a soup pot (8 quarts). Add vinegar and six quarts of water. Add carrots, celery, onions, parsley and thyme. Bring to a boil and then reduce heat to a simmer. Cook uncovered for 2 to 3 hours. Add string beans and chickpeas and cook an additional one-half hour. During cooking skim fat and foam from the top.

Remove bones and meat from soup to make meat dish. Serve soup over pasta.

**Meat Dish**

**Olive oil**

**Soup meat**

**1 onion, chopped**

**2 celery ribs**

Fry onion in olive oil.  Add celery and cook until celery is soft. Cut soup meat into small pieces and add to onion and celery mixture. Heat and serve with salad as a second dish with soup.

## Black Bean Soup

**1 pound black beans**

**1 onion (with 2 cloves)**

**1 bay leaf**

**Parsley sprig**

**1 medium onion, chopped**

**1 green pepper, chopped**

**2 garlic cloves, minced**

**¼ cup oil**

**1 teaspoon oregano**

**1 teaspoon sugar**

**1 teaspoon vinegar**

**1 8 ounce can tomato sauce**

**¼ cup dry sherry**

**Chopped onion for garnish**

Soak black beans overnight. To same water, add onion with cloves, bay leaf and parsley. Bring to a boil and cook beans until tender. Cook onion, green pepper and garlic in oil until soft. Add to the beans with the remaining ingredients and cook until thickened. Pour in dry sherry and serve with finely chopped raw onion sprinkled on top. (If a smooth soup is desired, puree in a blender.)

## Carrot and Orange Soup

4 tablespoons butter

2 cups onions, finely chopped

12 carrots, peeled and chopped

4 cups chicken stock

1 cup fresh orange juice

Orange zest, grated

Salt and pepper to taste

Melt butter in a pot. Add onions. Cover and cook over low heat until onions are tender. Add carrots and stock. Bring to a boil. Reduce heat. Cover and simmer until carrots are tender (about 30 minutes). Strain carrots, reserving stock liquid. Place carrots in blender. Add 1 cup chicken stock and blend until smooth. Return soup to pot; add orange juice and remaining reserved stock Add orange zest, salt and pepper. Simmer until heated through.

## Chickpea Soup

¼ cup olive oil

2 garlic cloves

¼ cup sliced onion

1 15.5 oz. can of chickpeas

½ pound egg noodles

Salt and pepper

Sauté garlic and onions in olive oil. Add chickpeas. Set aside. Cook egg noodles. Drain, saving liquid. Add egg noodles and enough liquid to make a soup consistency to the chick peas. Salt and pepper to taste. Serve.

**Note:**

I like to substitute dry chickpeas (garbanzo beans) for the canned beans. Soak one-third pound of dry beans overnight. Then, cook the beans until tender. Add beans to oil, garlic and onion mixture. Combine with cooked noodles. Salt and pepper to taste.

**Corn Chowder**

**4 slices raw bacon, diced**

**1 large onion, coarsely chopped**

**3 cups peeled and diced potatoes**

**3 cups water**

**4 tablespoons butter**

**¼ cup flour**

**2 cups milk**

**2 cups diced cooked ham**

**2 12 ounce cans whole kernel corn, undrained**

**2 teaspoons salt**

**¼ teaspoon pepper**

**2 tablespoons dried parsley flakes**

In a large skillet, cook bacon until almost crisp. Add onion and cook until soft. Add potatoes and water; cover and cook until potatoes are fork tender about 10 minutes. Melt butter in a heavy Dutch oven over low heat. Blend in flour.

Gradually add milk, stirring until mixture is thickened and smooth. To the white sauce, add the potato mixture, ham, corn, salt, pepper and parsley. Bring soup just to a boil but do not let it boil.  Soup may be frozen. Makes three quarts of chowder.

**Gazpacho Soup**

This recipe comes from my good friend Deanna Hoffman, my former Fairfield neighbor, who said this is actually a recipe from Gloria Vanderbilt.

**1 ½ cups Bloody Mary mix**

**1 teaspoon wine vinegar**

**1 teaspoon salad oil**

**½ teaspoon salt**

**1 tablespoon Worcestershire sauce**

**¼ cup chopped unpeeled cucumber**

**¼ cup chopped green and or red pepper**

**¼ chopped onion**

**1 cup chopped tomatoes**

**Croutons**

Mix Bloody Mary with oil, vinegar, Worcestershire sauce and salt. Put in refrigerator overnight. Serve with chopped vegetables and croutons served in individual bowls to allow for guests to freely choose vegetables and amounts to place in soup bowls.

**Lemon-Basil Squash Soup**

**2 tablespoons olive oil**

**1 large sweet onion, chopped**

**1 garlic clove, chopped**

**4 cups chicken stock or canned broth**

**3 medium-sized zucchini, ends removed, coarsely shredded**

**3 medium-sized summer squash, ends removed, coarsely shredded**

**1 medium-sized carrot, peeled and coarsely shredded**

**3 tablespoon coarsely shredded fresh basil**

**Grated rind of 1 lemon**

**Salt and pepper to taste**

Warm oil over low heat; add the onion and garlic and sauté for five minutes until the onion is translucent. Add the chicken broth, zucchini, squash, carrot, basil and lemon rind. Cook for five to eight minutes, until the vegetables are tender but still firm. Season to taste with salt and pepper.

## Meatless Minestrone or My Green Soup

One of my favorite cookbooks is "The Home Book of Italian Cooking," which was written by Angela Catanzaro in the 1960s. I recall that sometime in the 1970s, I bought this book and quickly it became one of my favorite "go-to" cookbooks in the kitchen. It is a small paperback cookbook; therefore, through the years the book became a little beat up, and I lost the first ten pages, including the cover. Fortunately, a few years ago, I found the same cookbook on Amazon and bought a copy. While perusing the book looking for a soup recipe, I came across a recipe titled, "Meatless Minestrone." It's an interesting combination of ingredients—all green.

I modified the recipe by adding a vegetable broth for more flavor, than just the water, which the recipe called for. I like the ingredients, which are all green, except the onion. Also, I realized in making the soup that cubed yellow potatoes could be a welcomed addition if you decide not to use pasta. Or instead of pasta, I have added cooked Pad Thai Rice Noodles to the soup.

**1 tablespoons olive oil**

**32 ounces vegetable broth**

**1 large onion**

**2 cups zucchini, diced**

**2 cups escarole, cut into 1-inch pieces**

**2 celery stalks with leaves, diced**

**¾ cup string beans cut into 1-inch pieces**

**1 knob kohlrabi, peeled and diced**

**Salt and pepper to taste**

**½ pound pasta, Ditalli, small shells or elbow macaroni, or instead of pasta - Pad Thai Rice**

**Noodles**

Cook onion in olive oil until translucent. Add vegetable broth and four cups of water. Bring to a boil. Reduce heat and add vegetables and seasonings. Cook on medium heat for 15 minutes. Cook pasta or noodles and add to soup.

**Minestrone Soup**

**1 cup white beans**

**1 tablespoon salt**

**Small piece of salt pork rind**

**2 strips bacon, diced**

**1 tablespoon olive oil**

**1 medium onion, sliced thin**

**1 large carrot, diced**

**1 stalk celery, diced**

**1 potato, diced**

**1 zucchini, diced**

**1 large tomato peeled, seeded and diced**

**1 teaspoon parsley, finely chopped**

**Salt and pepper to taste**

**1 medium-sized cabbage, sliced thin**

**1 garlic clove, finely chopped**

**Basil, 2 to 3 leaves**

**½ cup, uncooked pasta**

**½ cup chickpeas**

**1 ½ cup Parmesan cheese, grated**

Soak beans overnight in water. Drain the beans and put in large soup pot with 2 ½ quarts of water. Add salt and pork rind. Bring to a boil and simmer over low heat for 1 ½ hours. Meanwhile, cook bacon and onion in a saucepan with olive oil. Cook until the onion is done. Add carrot, celery, potato, and zucchini to the onion mixture. Cook for a few minutes and then add the tomato and parsley. Salt and pepper to taste. Cook the mixture briefly, stirring frequently. Add the mixture to the soup pot. Add cabbage, garlic and basil to the soup.

Simmer for 1 ½ hours or until soup is thick. In the last 20 minutes before the soup is done, add ½ cup uncooked pasta and ½ cup chickpeas (which had soaked in water overnight). Just before serving, stir in ½ cup parmesan cheese.

There are many variations of minestrone soup and a number of different vegetables can be added, such as fresh peas, string beans, turnips or eggplant, if desired.

## Pasta with Beans

¼ cup celery, chopped

¼ cup onion, chopped

1 tablespoon parsley

1 tablespoon oregano

1 garlic clove, minced

1 tablespoon olive oil

1 14.5 ounce can of cannellini beans

1 can condensed tomato soup

1 soup can of water

½ cup cooked elbow macaroni

½ teaspoon lemon juice

Cook celery, onion, parsley, oregano and garlic in oil until tender. Add remaining ingredients. Heat and stir.

## Pasta with Oil and Garlic

4 garlic cloves, chopped
1 cup olive oil
Parsley, chopped
Spaghetti or linguine
Red pepper, optional
Salt and pepper to taste
Anchovies, optional

Fry garlic in oil. Cook the pasta and drain, saving the water. Return the pasta to the pot Add the cooked garlic and chopped parsley (amount determined by preference). Add salt and pepper. Sprinkle red pepper on a serving if you prefer an added taste sensation.  Add some of the pasta water if the pasta is too dry.

This dish is good whether the pasta is spaghetti or linguine. I prefer linguine when serving the pasta with olive oil rather than a tomato sauce.  Add the anchovies to enhance the flavor.


**String Bean Soup**


This is another soup I remember my mother serving. It is a very easy soup to make and a very easy way for the family to eat vegetables.  The amount of each ingredient depends upon the number of servings and vegetable preference. I listed the following amounts for four servings.

There are two kinds of green beans that I select for this recipe. One is the traditional green bean that is available in all supermarkets. The other is the flat bean, usually available in specialty markets. I prefer the flat bean for, I believe, it is more flavorful.  The flat bean is also known as Helda bean or Romano beans. However, if unavailable the traditional string bean is fine.


**⅓ cup olive oil**

**4 garlic cloves,**

**1 ½ pounds string beans**

**4 medium-sized potatoes, either yellow or red, quartered**

**1 medium onion, sliced**

**2 tomatoes, quartered or cut in eighths**

**Salt and pepper to taste**

**Parmesan cheese, optional**

Brown garlic in olive oil. Add onion, tomatoes, potatoes and string beans. Stir to coat vegetables with oil. Add more oil if so desired. Cover with water, at least one or two inches above vegetables. Add salt and pepper.

Heats on top of stove until all vegetables are cooked. Serve vegetables in a bowl with sufficient amount of the soup water. Optional: sprinkle with Parmesan cheese.

## Zucchini Soup

**1 large zucchini, unpeeled and cut in chunks**

**2 small onions, sliced**

**2-3 cups chicken broth**

**Light cream**

**Salt and pepper**

**Dash of curry powder**

Simmer zucchini with onions and with enough chicken broth to cover vegetables until they are just cooked through. Blend in blender until creamy. Add light cream to make a desirable consistency. Add salt and pepper to taste. Serve hot or cold. Sprinkle with curry for variety.

# Matriarch of Italian Cuisine and the Family Table

Lidia Matticchio Bastianich is considered the matriarch of Italian cuisine. So many people flock to her appearances and buy her many books, including "Lidia's Family Table," and watch her popular PBS cooking series in which viewers have been introduced to her mother, Erminia; son, Joseph, a partner in her restaurants; daughter, Tanya, with whom Lidia launched an upscale tour company focusing on Italian food, wine and art; and her five grandchildren.

The family table concept underscores Lidia's philosophy about cooking and eating and the reason why she believes so many people attend her book-signings, buy her books and watch her TV cooking shows.

A few years ago, Lidia took time out from her busy schedule to share some thoughts with me about her popularity and the popularity of Italian cooking, which is deeply seated in the respect people have for the Italian culture, especially its art and music. Her fans believe in her philosophy – the importance of the family table.

This means that mealtime is the time for the family to gather and to share in the pleasures of conversation. She knows that the reality often is far different from what she espouses with "Lidia's Family Table" and her TV series. It is not uncommon today for a family member to be in the living room eating and watching TV or to be on a different schedule and not available to be home at dinnertime.

What do people say when they get an opportunity to meet Lidia one-on-one? Lidia said people thank her for communicating the Italian culture.

"It really touches me," said Lidia, who expressed surprise at the overwhelming turnouts for her book-signings. "They say, 'We love you. Our whole family watches you.'"

Lidia noted that they express such sentiments because they are tired of the way Italians have been portrayed on television and in the movies. "I bring forth my art and how I communicate it. I bring the culture of Italy, the importance of family and the importance of the generations. They love it." She described the family table as an opportunity for people "to nourish the body and nourish the soul." This is the message she provides with her food. It is part of her culture and part of a good life, she said.

"Society has put so much hype on the 'me' and 'my goals' and 'what am I achieving?' It's a lonely world out there, and it's hard to achieve the goals by yourself," Lidia said.

Lidia offered advice for people with busy schedules who face the challenge of cooking and entertaining. "Stick to your favorite recipes and things you've done before," she said. "Holidays are not the time to experiment. Stick to the simplest one." She suggested using the oven a lot, rather than cooking atop the stove to avoid mistakes.

Lidia said her greatest thrill is to be able to share her knowledge with others, especially when she gets e-mails from people who have used her recipes. "We don't know each other except through my books."

Why is Italian cooking so popular? Lidia said it makes sense in terms of nutrition, taste and preparation. The popularity stems from the concentration of flavors and seasonality and the way the meals are orchestrated. This is evident in her cookbooks, including "Lidia's Italian Table" and "Lidia's Italian-American Kitchen," among others.

When asked the difference between Italian and Italian-American cooking, the author, who immigrated to this country at age 12 from Istria, a region of northeastern Italy now part of Croatia, said Italian-American cooking is an adaptation of Italian cooking. In other words, the traditional Italian recipes were adapted in the United States when immigrants had to use ingredients that were available here. For example, she said, Italians do not eat meatballs with pasta and sauce, the way Italian-Americans do here; yet, in Italy, Italians make little meatballs to layer in lasagna or to drop into a pot of soup.

"Italian-American food," says Lidia, "has become a part of us—a slice of Americana. And that is what makes America, the piecing together of a slice of every culture, which in total makes a great whole."

# Biscuits, Breads and Pizza

## Baking Powder Biscuits

**2 cups flour**

**3 teaspoons baking powder**

**1 teaspoon salt**

**¼ cup shortening**

**⅔ cup milk**

Preheat oven to 450 degrees.

Mix flour, baking powder and salt together. Cut in shortening. Add milk and mix quickly. Knead for a few seconds on lightly floured board. Pat out to one-half inch thickness and cut with biscuit cutter. Place in greased pan close together for crust on top and bottom only (far apart if crust is desired on sides). Bake for 12 minutes. Makes 12 biscuits.

## Aunt Mary's Biscuits

**6 eggs**

**1 cup sugar**

**¾ cup oil**

**3 ½ cups flour**

**3 ½ teaspoons lemon extract**

**3 ¼ teaspoons baking powder**

**Chopped nuts – filberts, almonds or pecans**

Preheat oven to 375 degrees.

Mix all ingredients. Place dough on greased shallow pan ( 5" by 8 ½") Bake for 15 to 18 minutes. Cool and slice.

## Thelma's Lemon Bread

Note: Thelma was a friend of my mother, Aida ("Nana") Mallett. This is her recipe.

**¼ cup butter**

**1 cup sugar**

**2 eggs**

**Grated rind of one lemon**

**½ cup chopped nuts**

**½ cup flour**

**1 ½ teaspoons baking powder**

**½ tablespoon salt**

**½ cup milk**

Preheat oven to 350 degrees

Cream butter and sugar. Add eggs. Add lemon rind. Alternating with milk, add sifted dry ingredients (flour, baking powder, salt). Add nuts. Place in a 5" by 9" bread pan. Bake for one hour. Make a topping of 1/4 cup sugar, and juice of one lemon. Spread on a cooled cake.

**Enormous Popovers**

**1 cup sifted flour**

**½ teaspoon salt**

**1 cup milk**

**2 eggs**

Preheat oven to 425 degrees

Combine all ingredients into a batter. Brush heated custard cups with oil and pour batter into cups three-quarters full. Bake for 45 minutes.


**Snacking Pizza**

**1 package refrigerated biscuits (10)**

**½ cup tomato sauce**

**½ cup chopped mushrooms**

**½ cup grated mozzarella**

Preheat oven to 400 degrees

Flatten biscuits. Place on greased baking sheet. Spoon tomato sauce on biscuits. Top with mushrooms. Sprinkle cheese on top. Bake for eight minutes.

**Pizza the Easy Way**

**English Muffin Pizza**

**6 English Muffins, cut in half with a fork to preserve crevices**

**Tomato sauce, canned sauce is fine; homemade even better**

**Mozzarella or Muenster cheese (slices)**

**Olive oil**

**Oregano**

**Salt and pepper**

Preheat oven to 350 degrees

Spread tomato sauce on English muffins. Top with a slice of cheese. Drizzle olive oil on top. Season with oregano, salt and pepper. Bake in oven on a cookie sheet for approximately 20 minutes or until desired crispness.

**Naan Pizza**

**Naan bread, one round**

**Tomato sauce**

**Mozzarella cheese**

**Olive oil**

**Oregano**

**Salt and pepper**

Preheat oven to 400 degrees

The method is similar to making English muffin pizzas. Spread tomato sauce, cheese and seasonings on the Naan bread. Place directly on the rack in the oven. Cook for approximately 10 minutes or less. Check during baking to avoid overbaking. For a softer crust, place Naan on a cookie sheet to bake.

## Zucchini Bread

**1 cup walnuts, chopped into medium-sized pieces**

**2 eggs**

**1 ¼ cup sugar**

**1 cup vegetable oil**

**3 ½ cups unsifted all-purpose flour**

**1 ½ teaspoon baking soda**

**1 ½ teaspoon salt**

**1 teaspoon cinnamon**

**¾ teaspoon baking powder**

**2-3 cups grated zucchini (not peeled)**

**1 cup raisins**

**1 teaspoon vanilla**

Preheat oven to 350 degrees

Beat eggs and gradually beat in sugar. Add oil. Combine dry ingredients. Add to first mixture alternating with zucchini; Stir in raisins, walnuts and vanilla. Turn into two lightly floured loaf pans (9"x 5"). Bake about 55 minutes or until done.

# Sauces and Pesto

## Fresh Basil Pesto

This is a recipe from Nana Mallett's friend "Rose B."

**2 cups packed fresh basil leaves**

**2 large garlic cloves**

**½ cup pine nuts (or walnuts) optional**

**¾ cup grated Parmesan and Romano cheese mixed or only Romano.**

**⅓ cup olive oil.**

Using a food processor (or blender), combine basil and garlic. Blend to fine paste. Add pine nuts and cheese, and process until smooth. Add olive oil and mix until smooth and creamy. If paste is too thick, add ¼ warm water.

Transfer pesto to a jar. Cover surface of pesto with a film of olive oil. Seal jar with tight-fitting lid. Refrigerate. Stir oil into pesto before using.

## Hollandaise Sauce

**Place in blender:**

**4 egg yolks**

**2 tablespoons lemon juice**

**½ teaspoon salt**

**Tabasco sauce**

Turn blender on and off quickly. Heat ½ cup butter until hot. Turn blender to high and dribble butter in until thick.

## Norma's Puttanesca Sauce

This is cousin Norma's recipe that Nana Mallett had in her recipe file. It is just a few lines but it represents a very delicious sauce.

Brown chopped garlic in olive oil. Add chopped black olives, capers and a can of plum tomatoes. Simmer for approximately one hour and then serve over spaghetti.

## Tomato Sauce

When I make tomato sauce, I am reminded of my childhood with a pot of sauce cooking on the stove. It seemed that the sauce would be cooking early on a Sunday morning, even before I walked into the kitchen for breakfast. When I cook sauce it reminds me of my youth and the comfort of home. Even though I now am living alone, I still make my own tomato sauce whether it is for company or just me, for I find the process quite nostalgic. I am fortunate that my grandchildren Calum and Vivienne love pasta, so I get to make sauce and pasta a lot since they live nearby and frequently have dinner with me.

There are three recipes for tomato sauce, each with a slight variation in mixing and matching the different cans of tomatoes or fresh tomatoes. Choosing which recipe can depend upon preference, time and type of pasta selected. For example, do you want a light marinara sauce for spaghetti, or a thicker sauce for a pasta, such as rigatoni, ziti or shells?

Another decision in making tomato sauce is whether or not to add meat to the sauce. This decision involves the kind of meat—meatballs, sausage or braciole—with each adding a distinctive flavor to the sauce. You can make sauce with one, two or even three kinds of meat.

## Basic Marinara Sauce

**1 14 ounce can plum tomatoes**

**Basil**

**1 small onion (optional)**

**1 garlic clove**

**Olive oil**

**Salt and pepper to taste**

Sauté garlic in olive oil and cook until garlic becomes light brown. Add onions and cook until onions become translucent. Place tomatoes in a blender and blend until smooth or squeeze tomatoes by hand and place with liquid into the pot with the oil, garlic and onion. Add basil, salt and pepper and cook on top of stove for one hour and 15 minutes.

## Variation of Basic Marinara Sauce

**1  8 ounce can of tomato paste**

**1 8- ounce can of tomato sauce**

**1 28 -ounce can of peeled tomatoes or 2-3 pounds of fresh plum tomatoes**

**1 28-ounce can crushed tomatoes**

**Garlic**

**Olive oil**

**Onion (optional)**

**Basil**

**Salt and pepper to taste**

Brown garlic in olive oil and sauté. Add onion (optional) and cook until translucent. Add can of tomato paste. Put water in can and add to pot. Simmer slowly for a few minutes. Put can of tomatoes in a blender and blend or place tomatoes in pot and break up tomatoes with a fork.

If using fresh plum tomatoes, chop up tomatoes and place in pot. Stir and cook a few minutes. Add can of tomato sauce. Add basil, salt and pepper. Blend all ingredients in pot and cook sauce for approximately one and a half hours. (I like to cook it even longer, on simmer) Stir frequently. This is the part that I find therapeutic, actually. It calms me and brings back memories of childhood. Serve over cooked pasta. Serves four.

**Variations with Meat Added to Sauce**

**Sausage**

**1 pound sweet sausage.**

Brown sausage in a skillet until cooked. Drain on paper towel. Add to sauce.

**Meatballs**

**1 ½ pound mixture of chopped sirloin beef, chopped pork and chopped veal**

**½ cup breadcrumbs**

**½ cup grated parmesan cheese**

**¼ to ½ cup parsley, chopped**

**1 onion, chopped**

**1 egg**

**Salt and pepper to taste**

Combine all ingredients and form into small balls. Fry in vegetable oil. Place in sauce for last 20 minutes of cooking sauce.

**Braciole**

**Cube steaks - approximately 3-4 inch squares**

**Garlic, minced**

**Parsley**

**Grated Parmesan cheese**

**Salt and pepper to taste**

Make a mixture of the raw minced garlic, parsley, Parmesan cheese. Add salt and pepper to taste. Place mixture on top of each cube steak. Roll up each piece. Tie with string or fasten with toothpicks to keep roll from unravelling. Fry each roll and then add to tomato sauce. Cook in sauce for approximately one-half hour.

# Putting Color in Your Life

Carol Simontacchi wants to put more color in people's lives. A clinical nutritionist, Simontacchi believes the more colorful the food, the better the nutritional value.

"It's in the colors that you find the benefit," said the author of "Your Fat is Not Your Fault" and "The Crazy Makers: How the Food Industry is Destroying Our Brains and Harming Our Children."

Simontacchi says it is common for people to think that a plate of iceberg lettuce topped with a heaping tablespoon of Thousand Islands dressing is a salad.

Not so. Think color! A salad is a serving of "several kinds of vegetables — romaine lettuce, peppers, onions, cabbage," says the nutritionist. She may toss this with olive oil, balsamic vinegar and kosher salt or "If I want my food to be really flavorful, I add some herbs.

"Flavor is important because we should enjoy our food and be inspired to eat it. If you're not enjoying the food, you'll likely not stay on the program."

The program is Wings: Weight Success for a Lifetime™, a holistic approach to weight success, health and wellness that Simontacchi created.  It is an educationally based program to control weight, taught by an instructor or offered in a home-study format. Weight management involves the endocrine system, digestive system and nervous system—in short, the whole body. It's more than "a mouth issue," says Simontacchi, noting two lasting images come to mind for most people when they think about dieting: "temporary and starvation."

Her program is a way of life—a way to shop for groceries, a way of cooking and eating and a way of listening to your body. It's not a diet in which weight loss is followed by weight gain and health problems.

Wings is a starting point. Simontacci calls it a "journey." Weight maintenance is a lifestyle. Through education and awareness, Simontacci wants people to realize that they can "lose weight forever and increase health and vitality."

With all the interest in healthy food and a healthy lifestyle, why is America so fat? And why are we getting fatter every year?"

Simontacchi says the issues are complex. They relate to eating the proper nutritional foods; genetics; and the body's overall health, which affects the endocrine system, the digestive system and elimination. Allergies, hormones, stress and prescription drugs, even environmental factors, may factor into weight balance and control.

The author says: "Logic tells us if we clean up our diets and eat pure foods, including 30-40 grams of fiber a day, drink 8 to 10 glasses of water and avoid synthetic chemicals as a much as possible, our bodies will not have to build storage deposits on our hips and bellies."

Simontacchi acknowledges that losing weight and keeping the weight off is a very complex issue which can lead to complex results, such as depression and lack of energy.

She advises readers to clean out the refrigerator and cabinets to remove all non-foods—food-like products synthesized in some chemist's lab; i.e. carbonated beverages, packaged cereals, simulated fruit beverages, processed sugars; packaged foods; potato and corn chips; and all other convenient foods.

Simontacchi offers "Carol's Rules for Healthy Eating":
- Never eat anything that comes with instructions
- Never eat anything that comes in a box, a can, or a wrapper.
- Never eat anything white (Potatoes are brown; rice is beige, cauliflower is cream colored, and ice cream is nasty!).
- Never eat anything you can't spell or pronounce.
- Never eat anything you just can't live without (you're probably allergic to it).

Simontacchi wasn't born with this knowledge. She was born into a family with a mother who would pick the green string beans in her garden; simmer them for hours; and serve them with bacon fat.

"I really ate horrible food. I was sick a lot. I had a skin problem. I was seriously depressed."

Her depression continued into her 20s when her boss at the

time gave her a copy of *Prevention* magazine to help her address her problems.

"I got off a lot of the sugar I was eating. I started eating real food." She became interested in nutrition, which eventually led to her certification in nutrition.

Simontacchi distressed by the increase in juvenile obesity, which is due to poor nutrition and a sedentary existence fueled by the popularity of television-watching and fast-food eating.

"Children eat less than two daily portions of fruit and vegetables and a quarter of the servings is French fries," she says.

The nutritionist faults public education for its contribution to poor eating. On one hand, the schools preach the importance of the basic food groups; on the other hand, cafeteria food lacks nutrition and the schools allow the selling of carbonated soft drinks in the schools' vending machines

Simontacchi advises:

"If you are going to lose weight and keep it off, you're going to have to turn your back on the American food culture and learn to eat your ancestral diet. Your grandparents enjoyed moderate amounts of protein foods, small amounts of seasonal fruits, and lots of vegetables washed down with clean water. They ate what was in season at the time, freshly harvested. Some foods, like winter squash, potatoes, carrots, and a few other fruits and vegetables that could be stored in a cellar were saved for the winter; everything else was eaten as soon as it was picked from the field or the garden.

"This is the type of diet your body was designed to eat, and it will bring your waistline back under control...trust me, it is the diet your body was meant to eat, and your body will reward you by dropping those excess pounds and adding years of vital health to your life."

# Vegetables and Sides

## Marinade for Vegetables

**1 cup vinegar, wine and distilled**

**1 cup oil**

**1 teaspoon garlic powder**

**1 teaspoon salt**

**1 teaspoon dill weed**

**1 tablespoon sugar**

Blend all ingredients and chill before serving

## Stuffed Artichokes

A person either likes the taste of an artichoke or not. You cannot fake enjoying this vegetable. And if you like the taste, it is quite a treat to sit down and pick off each stuffed leaf, scrap your teeth along the leaf to capture the mix of artichoke and stuffing in your mouth. I don't know how other people stuff their artichokes, but this is the recipe that I remember my mother making. Therefore, I set down the ingredients and method of cooking and eating from memory.

I am listing the ingredients; however, the amount of each ingredient depends upon the number of artichokes to be stuffed and individual taste for the ingredients.

In selecting an artichoke, look for artichokes with leaves that are snug to the core of the artichoke. For example, the more open the leaves are, the less flavorful and tougher. At times, I've been fortunate to find large green globes with the leaves that look as if they have been painted on the artichoke. If you're lucky, you can find these artichokes in stores such as Whole Foods. And if you're lucky, they may be on sale. If not, they may still be worth the purchase.

**Artichokes**

**Breadcrumbs**

**Parsley**

**Parmesan cheese**

**Garlic powder**

**Salt and pepper**

**Olive oil**

Soak the artichokes in a bowl of water. As you soak the artichokes, open up the leaves so that you can stuff each leaf. Cut off the stem of each artichoke and snip off the tip of each leaf (straight across) to eliminate the prickly part.

Mix the ingredients together to form a paste. Stuff each leaf with a teaspoon of filling. Place the artichokes in a pot. Fill the pot with water sufficient enough to steam the artichokes, but not drown them in water. The artichokes are done when you can easily pull away a leaf from the artichoke.   Eat the artichokes by taking off a leaf, one at a time. Notice that the leaves are tougher as you get to the lower part of the artichoke. After all the leaves are pulled, slice off the bottom part –the heart, which is very tasty to eat. Avoid eating the "hairy" part.

**Maria's Fresh Asparagus with Vinaigrette**

**Fresh asparagus**

**3 tablespoons wine vinegar**

**1 ½ Dijon mustard**

**8 tablespoons olive oil**

**Chopped parsley**

**Salt and pepper**

Cook asparagus in boiling salted water for eight minutes. Drain and cool. Mix remaining ingredients and drizzle on the asparagus


**Banana Fritters**

**1 cup flour**

**1 tablespoon sugar**

**¼ teaspoon salt**

**1 egg**

**¼ cup milk**

**3 bananas, mashed**

**1 tablespoon lemon juice**

**Cinnamon and Confectioner's sugar for topping**

Combine flour, sugar and salt. Beat egg and add to milk. Combine flour and egg mixtures. Stir in bananas and lemon juice. Fill a small scoop of mixture to form pancakes in frying pan with heated oil. Fry fritters on both sides. Sprinkle confectioner's sugar and cinnamon on top.


## Aunt Mary's Stuffed Cabbage

**2 pounds pork, chopped**

**1 ½ cups rice (uncooked)**

**Onions**

**Salt and pepper**

**Cabbage leaves**

**Tomato sauce**

Preheat oven to 350 degrees.

Steam cabbage. Cook rice. Sauté onions. Mix, onions, pork, and rice. Stuff cabbage leaves and place in pan. Pour tomato sauce over the cabbage. Bake for one hour.


## Cabbage Rolls

**1 onion**

**1 tablespoon fat**

**1 cup cooked rice**

**½ pound chopped beef**

**Salt and pepper**

**1 head cabbage**

**2 beef bouillon cubes**

**1 cup hot water**

**1 can or 2 small cans tomato sauce**

Preheat oven to 350 degrees

Fry onions in fat until golden. Add meat and brown. Add cooked rice. Season with salt and pepper.  Place cabbage in boiling water. Cover and cook to separate the leaves. Spoonful sautéd meat and rice on each leaf.  Wrap. Place in pan. Dissolve beef bouillon and tomato sauce together. Pour over cabbage rolls.  Bake covered for one hour.

**Cole Slaw**

**1 large head of cabbage**

**2 medium onions**

**¾ cup sugar**

**Chop cabbage and onions. Add sugar and mix**

Boil:

**¾ cup white vinegar**

**¾ cup salad oil**

**1 tbs. salt**

**2 tsp. sugar**

**1 tsp. dry mustard**

**1 tsp. celery seed**

Immediately pour mixture over the chopped cabbage and onions. Refrigerate. (This cole slaw will keep for at least a week. The longer it sets, the better it tastes.)

## Corn Fritters

My mother, Nana Mallett, would make these corn fritters and serve with stewed tomatoes and applesauce. Somehow, I suspect it was one of those evenings when she did not have much food to cook or maybe energy to be creative. It is a good meal to have, for it includes the kinds of ingredients one would probably have on the shelf.

**1 can creamed corn**

**2 tablespoons cooking oil**

**1 egg**

**1 cup flour**

**1 teaspoon baking powder**

Mix together the creamed corn, egg, flour and baking powder. Drop by tablespoon into oil in heated frying pan. Fry on both sides.

## Chinese Eggplant

**1 eggplant cubed**

**6 black mushrooms, soaked and diced**

**2 green peppers, diced**

**2 tablespoons chili paste**

½ tablespoon dark soy sauce

½ tablespoon light soy sauce

2 tablespoons wine

1 tablespoon red vinegar

½ teaspoon MSG

2 teaspoons sugar

1 teaspoon salt


Mix together chili paste, soy sauce, wine, vinegar, MSG, sugar and salt. Cook eggplant in oil for five minutes. Drain. Cook mushrooms and peppers for two minutes in 2 tablespoons of oil. Add eggplant and cook five minutes; add ½ cup water. Stir. Add chili mixture.


## Stuffed Escarole

This recipe comes from the book I wrote in 2001, titled "Gioacchino: Memoir of an Italian Immigrant." It is a biography of Jack DiScala, a prominent real estate developer in Norwalk, Connecticut, who passed away in 2006 at the age of 94. In writing his biography, in which he immigrated to this country from his native Ischia, an island off the coast of Naples, I included a sampling of recipes that Jack enjoyed cooking with his wife, Mary, of 64 years. When I make stuffed escarole, I think of the DiScala family and the many professional years I enjoyed working as a public relations consultant in promoting the M.F. DiScala Company, Inc.

In my introduction to the DiScala book, I noted that I was drawn to the DiScalas, for we not only share the same Italian heritage, but also their family values along with their spirit, energy and ambition.

**4 tablespoons parsley, chopped**

**4 garlic cloves, cut in half**

**½ cup onions**

**½ cup pignoli nuts**

**½ cup olive oil**

**Salt to taste**

**Head of escarole.**

Wash and take apart a head of escarole and place in a pot. I like to cut off the base of the escarole in order to keep the escarole's round shape in the pot. Mix together the parsley, garlic, raisins, pignoli nuts, olive oil and salt. Place spoonfuls of the mixture among the layers of the escarole. Cook covered until the escarole leaves appear cooked.


**Stuffed Grape Leaves**

**Grape leaves**

**1 cup rice**

**3 pounds onions**

**1 cup olive oil**

**Parsley, chopped**

**Salt and pepper to taste**

**1 lemon**

Cook rice. Fry onions in oil until soft. Add rice. Stir five minutes. Add parsley. Add salt and pepper. Cool. Fill leaves and place in pot. Add 1 ½ cups boiling water in the pot. Put dish on top of leaves. Bring to a boil again and simmer 20 minutes. Squeeze lemon over grape leaves. Serve cold.

**Note:** This recipe comes from my mother-in-law. She was of Armenian heritage, but lived in Turkey before immigrating to the U.S., I believe in the 1930s or before. She taught me how to stuff grape leaves, which she usually would pick herself. While it is a delicious complement to a meal, it is very tedious to make.

**Mushrooms and Ham on Toast**

**1 pound mushrooms**

**½ stick butter**

**1 onion, chopped**

**Salt and pepper**

**1 tablespoon lemon juice**

**¼ teaspoon paprika**

**12 ounces sour cream**

**Ham slices**

**Toast**

Sauté mushrooms and onions in butter. Add salt and pepper, lemon juice, paprika, sour cream. Heat, but do not boil. Serve over ham on toast. Sprinkle with parsley.

## Stuffed Peppers I

These are two recipes for stuffed peppers. My mother used to make the first recipe with the Italian frying peppers and my mother-in-law the second recipe with green bell peppers.

**6 Italian frying peppers (Cubanelle peppers)**

**1 ½ cups breadcrumbs**

**⅓ cup capers**

**½ cup parsley**

**⅓ cup oil cured black olives, sliced**

**Garlic powder to taste**

**Salt and pepper to taste**

**Olive oil**

**Wine vinegar**

Preheat 350 degree oven

Slice off top of each Cubanelle pepper. Scoop out thin membrane and seeds. Mix bread crumbs, capers, parsley, olives, garlic powder, salt and pepper. Add olive oil and vinegar to moisten mixture. Fill each pepper with mixture. Place in oven proof pan. Sprinkle additional olive oil and vinegar over peppers. Bake in oven until peppers are done (Approximately one-half hour). Turn over peppers after 15 minutes. Peppers can be served hot or cold.

## Stuffed Peppers II

**4 green bell peppers**

**1 pound ground sirloin beef**

**½ bunch parsley, chopped**

**½ cup white rice, uncooked**

**8 ounce can tomato sauce**

**Salt and pepper to taste**

Slice off top of each pepper. Save tops. Scoop out membrane. Mix together the remaining ingredients (save 2 ounces of the tomato sauce). Fill each pepper with the mixture. Top each pepper with pepper slice. Place peppers in pot. Add water to pot. (approximately halfway up pepper). Pour remaining tomato sauce into water.

Spoon water/sauce over peppers to moisten. Cook atop stove until peppers are done. (Approximately 30 to 45 minutes). Check cooking to make sure water does not evaporate.

## Potato Latkes

**6 medium- size potatoes**

**2 eggs, slightly beaten**

**1 tablespoon flour**

**1 teaspoon salt**

**Dash of pepper**

**¼ teaspoon baking powder**

Peel and grate potatoes. Place in strainer and let water run through for a few seconds. Place in bowl after thoroughly draining. Stir in eggs. Add other ingredients. Drop by spoonful onto a hot well-greased skillet. Brown on both sides. Drain on absorbent paper. Serve hot with applesauce. Serves 4 to 6.

## Baked Pumpkin Seeds

**2 cups pumpkin seeds**

**½ tablespoons melted butter**

**1 teaspoon Worcestershire sauce**

Preheat oven to 250 degrees.

Combine butter and sauce and pour over pumpkin seeds. Bake for one hour.

## Spinach Pie

**2 pounds ricotta**

**2 eggs**

**½ cup grated cheese**

**½ pound grated mozzarella**

**2 packages frozen spinach (chopped)**

**Salt and pepper**

Preheat oven to 350 degrees

Defrost and drain spinach. Mix cheeses and eggs. Add spinach and bake in pie dish for one hour.

## Green Tomatoes

Wash and cut tomatoes in pieces. Pack jar with tomatoes with slivers of garlic and dill added. Fill jar with the following mixture: ½ water, ½ white vinegar, salt and pickling spices. Let jar stand uncovered for four days. Each day cover jar and shake to mix. Seal and keep refrigerated.

## Stewed Tomatoes

**5 medium tomatoes**

**3 slices of bread**

**Butter**

**Salt and pepper**

**Breadcrumbs**

Preheat oven to 350 degrees

Mash tomatoes with a fork. Add pieces of bread and mix into the tomatoes. Dart with butter. Add salt and pepper. Top with bread crumbs. Bake in oven until liquid is absorbed.

## Stuffing for Chicken or Turkey

(Amounts of ingredients are determined by the size of the bird and personal preference.)

**Bread stuffing (packaged, i.e. Pepperidge Farm)**

**Celery, diced**

**Onion, diced**

**Sweet Italian sausage (bulk}, cooked**

**Chicken broth**

**Vegetable oil**

**Poultry seasoning**

Preheat oven to 350 degrees

Cook onions in oil until translucent. Add celery. Add chicken broth (enough to cover celery and to cook until soft). Shut heat. Add sausage to onion and celery mixture. (If bulk sausage is unavailable buy sausage links and remove sausage from casing). Add bread stuffing. Add additional chicken broth to reach desired consistency of stuffing — not too soft and not to dry. Add poultry seasoning — gently. Do not overpower flavor of stuffing. Test for desired flavor.

Place stuffing in baking dish and bake in 350-degree oven for approximately 20 to 30 minutes. Stuffing can also be placed in chicken or turkey, but bird must go into the oven immediately. Do not let stuffed uncooked bird sit out of oven. If not comfortable with this process, then cook all stuffing separately in oven.

## Baked Zucchini

6 small zucchini sliced

1 large onion, sliced

¼ cup red vinegar

1 cup salad oil

2 packets of Good Seasoning Italian Dressing Mix

1 cup Parmesan cheese

Aluminum foil

Heat oven to 400 degrees.

Mix zucchini and onion. Sprinkle with Good Seasoning and pour vinegar and oil over mixture. Place on a sheet of aluminum foil. Close to make a packet shape allowing air space. Bake on cookie sheet for 45 minutes.

## Stuffed Zucchini

1 large green zucchini

2 large onions, diced

1 pound sweet Italian sausage, ground

2 cups breadcrumbs

8 ounces mushrooms, sliced

Poultry seasoning, to taste

Salt and pepper to taste

1 cup butter

**1 egg beaten**

Preheat oven to 350 degrees

Cook diced onions and sliced mushrooms in melted butter until soft. Pour contents into a large mixing bowl. Cook sausage and set aside. Slice zucchini lengthwise; scoop out seeds and place cut side up in a roasting pan. Add ¼ inch water. Combine bread crumbs with onions and mushrooms. Add egg, sausage and seasonings. Mix thoroughly. Stuff zucchini with mixture. Roast in oven until lightly browned, about 30 to 45 minutes.

## Stuffed Zucchini II

**1 ½ pounds small zucchini**

**1 ½ cup breadcrumbs**

**½ cup grated processed American cheese**

**¼ cup minced onion**

**1 tablespoon parsley, chopped**

**2 eggs, beaten**

**2 tablespoons butter**

Preheat oven to 350 degrees

Wash zucchini. Cut off ends Place in one-inch pot of boiling water with salt, covered for about 5 minutes. Remove zucchini from pot. Cut squash in half lengthwise. With tip of spoon remove squash from shells. Chop into small pieces. Combine zucchini with breadcrumbs and remaining ingredients, except butter. Pile mixture lightly into zucchini shells. Dot with butter. Bake in oven until done.

## Zucchini Crescent Pie

**4 cups thinly sliced unpeeled zucchini**

**1 cup coarsely chopped onion**

**½ cup butter**

**½ cup chopped parsley or 2 tablespoons parsley flakes**

**½ teaspoon salt**

**½ teaspoon black pepper**

**¼ teaspoon garlic powder**

**¼ teaspoon sweet basil leaves**

**¼ teaspoon oregano**

**2 eggs well beaten**

**8 ounces (2 cups) shredded Muenster or mozzarella cheese**

**1 8-ounce can refrigerated crescent dinner rolls.**

**2 teaspoons Dijon or prepared mustard**

Preheat oven to 375 degrees

In a 10-inch skillet, cook zucchini and onions in butter until tender, about 10 minutes. Stir in parsley and seasonings. In a large bowl, blend eggs and cheese. Stir in vegetable mixture. Separate dough into eight triangles. Place in ungreased 11-inch quiche pan or 10-inch pie pan or 12" x 8" baking dish. Press rolls over bottom and up sides to form crust. Spread crust with mustard. Pour vegetable mixture evenly into crust.

Bake for 18 to 20 minutes or until knife inserted near center comes out clean. If crust becomes too brown, cover with foil during last 10 minutes of baking. Let stand 10 minutes before serving. Serves six.


## Zucchini Fritters

**4 cups grated unpeeled zucchini**

**2 eggs, lightly beaten**

**¼ cup chopped parsley**

**1 tablespoon grated lemon zest**

**2 tablespoons grated Parmesan cheese**

**1 cup flour**

**1 teaspoon baking powder**

**Salt and pepper to taste**

**Oil for frying**

Combine the zucchini, eggs, parsley, lemon zest, Parmesan, flour, baking powder, salt and pepper. Beat lightly. Drop tablespoons of batter into heated oil in a frying pan. Fry fritter on each side until golden brown.


## Zucchini, Hominy and Chickpeas Bake

**2 tablespoons flour**

**2 teaspoons chili powder**

**1 teaspoon salt**

**2 medium zucchini sliced**

**2 medium tomatoes sliced**

**1 large onion sliced thin**

**1 medium green pepper cut into strips**

**1 15 ounce can hominy, drained**

**1 16 ounce can chickpeas, drained**

**1 cup shredded cheddar cheese**

Preheat oven to 350 degrees

Mix flour, chili powder and salt. Set aside. In greased three-quart casserole layer one-half zucchini, tomatoes, onion, green peppers, hominy, chickpeas, flour mixture and cheese. Repeat. Cover and bake oven for one hour and 20 minutes or until tender.


**Zucchini Pie**

**3 cups grated and cubed zucchini**

**1 onion diced**

**1 cup Bisquick**

**4 eggs**

**½ cup oil**

**½ cup grated Parmesan cheese**

**½ cup basil**

**1 teaspoon parsley**

¼ teaspoon pepper

¼ teaspoon salt

Preheat oven to 350 degrees

Mix together all ingredients. Place in a greased pie plate. Bake 30 to 35 minutes or until done.


## Zucchini Ribbons with Tomatoes and Black Olives

**2 pounds zucchini**

**1 ½ tablespoons olive oil**

**Salt, to taste**

**1 clove garlic, crushed**

**1 plum tomato, cored and diced**

**¼ cup small black olives, pitted**

**8 basil leaves, cut into fine strips**

**½ cup grated Parmesan cheese**

Peel the zucchini lengthwise into ribbons. Peel the sides just until you reach the inner core of seeds. Discard seeds. Sprinkle zucchini strips with salt and set aside. Use your hands to squeeze the excess juices from the zucchini.

 Heat oil in large skillet and brown garlic. Discard garlic. Add the zucchini and tomato. Cook for 2 or 3 minutes, until zucchini softens. Add the olives and basil. Serve with sprinkled parmesan cheese.

## Zucchini Stir Fry

**2 slices bacon, diced**

**1 green onion, sliced**

**3 medium zucchini, sliced diagonally**

**½ cup chicken broth**

**1 teaspoon cornstarch**

**1 teaspoon soy sauce**

**½ teaspoon salt**

**2 teaspoons cold water**

Cook bacon until crisp in a heavy saucepan or skillet. Drain on paper towels. Reserve drippings. Return 2 tablespoons drippings to pan and heat. Add onion and zucchini and toss, stirring constantly until vegetables are shiny. Pour in chicken broth; cover pan and steam vegetables about three minutes. Blend remaining ingredients and add to pan. Stir and heat to boiling. Turn into serving dishes and top with bacon bits. Makes four servings.

# Eggs and Cheese

## My Mother's Deviled Eggs

6 eggs

¼ cup salad dressing

1 teaspoon vinegar

1 teaspoon prepared mustard

Salt and pepper to taste

or

5 eggs

2 tablespoons mayonnaise

2 tablespoons chopped black olives

2 teaspoons vinegar

1 teaspoon prepared mustard

Salt and pepper to taste

**Additional suggested ingredients: horseradish, anchovies, parsley, chopped onion, chives, stuffed green olives, crumbled crisp cooked bacon**

Cook eggs until they are hard-boiled. Cut in half. Remove yolks and mash with ingredients of choice and then refill eggs. Optional: Sprinkle with paprika. Chill.

## Bacon Quiche

**9-inch unbaked pie shell**

**6 pieces of bacon**

**1 onion**

**3 eggs**

**1 yolk**

**1 cup heavy cream**

**2 cups milk**

**½ teaspoon salt**

**Dash of pepper**

**Pinch of nutmeg**

**⅔ cup grated Swiss or Gruyere cheese**

Preheat oven to 350 degrees.

Brown pie shell. Broil bacon. Drain, crumble and place in bottom of pie shell. Sauté onion and add to pie shell. Beat eggs and yolk. Add cream, milk, salt, pepper, nutmeg and cheese. Pour into shell. Bake for 25 to 30 minutes (until knife comes out clean).

## Quiche Lorraine

**One 9-inch unbaked pie shell**

**6 slices bacon, cooked and crushed**

**8 ounces Swiss cheese grated**

**3 eggs**

**1 ½ cups light cream or half and half**

**½ teaspoon salt**

**⅛ teaspoon pepper**

**1 tablespoon butter**

Preheat oven to 375 degrees

Spread bacon and cheese in bottom of pie shell. In mixing bowl, beat eggs slightly. Add cream, salt and pepper. Beat to combine. Pour into shell. Break butter into small pieces over filling. Bake for 35 to 40 minutes until knife comes clean. Let stand 10 minutes before cutting.

# Bittman Encourages Others to Eat Healthy

In an informative, entertaining and, at times, eye-opening talk a few years ago, Mark Bittman, former writer of "The Minimalist" column for "The New York Times," espoused the message presented in his 2009 book, "Food Matters: A Guide to Conscious Eating." He said, "Eating fewer animals and less junk food and super-refined carbohydrates" can improve people's health as well as the planet's while changing livestock production and lowering the cost of a household's food budget.

Author of "How to Cook Everything," Bittman's talk was part of WSHU's live lecture series, "Join the Conversation," which puts noted speakers together with public radio listeners for engaging thought-provoking discussions.

Bittman did not disappoint. He had his audience from his first statistic culled from a report from the United Nations Food and Agriculture Organization called, "Livestock's Long Shadow." The report notes that "global livestock production is responsible for 18 percent of greenhouse gases. When Bittman first read this statistic, he became concerned about animal production: the way animals are raised, the quality of meat and the impact on people's diets. He concluded that simple diet changes could not only improve health but also "help stop global warming."

At the same time, Bittman had gained weight, developed sleep apnea and high cholesterol, and his knees were giving out.

In his book, he writes, "I could see the writing on the wall; industrial meat production had gone beyond distasteful and alienating right through to disgusting and dangerous; traditional, natural ingredients were becoming more and more rare; and respectable scientific studies were all pointing in the same general directions."

Bittman's message is to eat more vegetables, fruits, legumes and whole grains. He advises that people can do this without "suffering or giving up all the food you love."

Bittman said individuals eat three pounds of food a day. Of this, two pounds are animal products, a half-pound is junk food and the remaining is fruit and vegetables. He wants people to change the equation, and suggests visualizing a seesaw. On one side is a pile of animal products and junk foods and the other is the fruit, vegetables, legumes and whole grains. The goal is to bring balance to one's eating habits.

"You don't have to eat only fruit and vegetables to be better; only more fruit and vegetables to be better. You can eat meat, cheese, processed food; just eat less and in increments." In order to change eating habits, he suggests people begin as slowly as once a week. Substitute a bowl of oatmeal for bacon and eggs.

"Figure out a way to bring better stuff home and cook it simply. Shift the balance of food,": said Bittman, who told audience members that he did not want to tell them how to change their eating habits, but just do something to wean away from the number of animal products and junk food they were consuming.

He follows the healthy eating path until "the sun goes down." In his book, he writes that he started eating a diet that was nearly "vegan until six." Until dinnertime, he ate almost no animal products at all. "At dinner, I always had a sizable meal including animal products, bread, dessert, wine, you name it, and sometimes, a salad and a bowl of soup- whatever I wanted."

Two years into his way of eating, Bittman lost 35 pounds, the high cholesterol has gone down and his apnea disappeared. He admits he now has "this self-righteous smug about me."

Throughout his book and in his talk, Bittman emphasized that he is not advocating a new diet, but "a change in focus, away from the 20th century style of gorging and back to something saner, more traditional, and less manufactured."

"Food Matters" offers tips on sane shopping, pantry stocking and restaurant menu navigation. He lays out a month's worth of meal plans and includes more than 75 recipes. He offers basic advice from steaming vegetables, to cooking beans, tomato sauce and soups.

His book offers the simple approach to getting back to home cooking. His book "is not about ignoring the troubles of the world when getting back to the kitchen; it's about the troubles of the world and getting back to the cooking."

# Pasta and Rice

## Baked Macaroni

**2 cups elbow macaroni**

**2 tablespoons margarine or butter**

**Cubed cheddar cheese**

**Milk**

**Salt and pepper**

**Breadcrumbs**

Preheat oven to 350 degrees.

Cook macaroni and place in a buttered 9" by 13" Pyrex dish. Spot with margarine or butter. Add cubed cheese throughout dish. Cover with milk. Add salt and pepper. Sprinkle with breadcrumbs. Bake until the milk is absorbed.

## My Mother's Baked Macaroni and Cheese

**½ cup elbow macaroni**

**3 tablespoons butter**

**3 tablespoons flour**

**2 cups milk**

**½ teaspoon salt**

**Dash of pepper**

**2 cups shredded mild cheddar cheese**

Preheat oven to 350 degrees

Cook macaroni and set aside. Melt butter in a pan. Blend in flour. Add milk and cook until thick. Add salt and pepper and cheese until cheese is melted. Mix with cooked macaroni. Place in a 1 ½ quart casserole dish. Sprinkle with dry bread crumbs. Bake for 45 minutes or until bubbly.

## Fettuccine Alfredo

**1 pound Fettuccine**

**6 tablespoons butter**

**½ cup Parmesan cheese**

**½ cup Gruyere cheese**

**½ cup heavy cream**

Cook Fettuccine. Melt butter and add to Fettuccine. Add cheeses and cream.

## Lasagna

My recipe for lasagna actually came from my sister-law-Barbara, whose ethnicity was Polish. I don't recall my mother making lasagna so Barbara gave me a copy of her own recipe, which I really like. However, during one of my visits to my cousin Bob, who lives in South Carolina now, near his daughter, I learned that the recipe I have is quite different than the Italian way of making lasagna, at least the way that the Butta family makes it.

 My recipe calls for chopped beef and sausage, whereas, Bob and his daughter Susan make little meatballs which they layer with the cheese and ribbons of lasagna. While I greatly admired their meticulous manner in assembling all the ingredients that go into this delicious dish, I choose to stay with the way I make the popular holiday meal. Incidentally, lasagna is so delicious that one does not have to wait for a holiday to enjoy making and eating it.

**3 cloves of garlic finely chopped**

**1 onion chopped**

**3 28 ounce cans plum tomatoes**

**1 14 ounce can of tomato sauce**

**2  6 ounce cans of tomato paste**

**2 lbs. lasagna**

**3 lbs. container of ricotta cheese**

**1 lb. mozzarella**

**1 egg**

**2-3 cups grated cheese**

**Parsley**

**Ground pepper**

**1 ½ lbs. ground sausage**

**1 ½lbs.  ground sirloin beef**

Preheat oven to 350 degrees

Make tomato sauce with the plum tomatoes, tomato sauce and tomato paste.  Set aside.   Cook pasta and set aside.  Beat egg and fold into ricotta. Add grated cheese, parsley and ground pepper to the ricotta.  Brown garlic and onion. Add sausage and beef to the garlic and onion and cook until the meat is done.  Then place meat mixture into tomato sauce.

 Begin layering the ingredients in a 9" by 13" baking pan. (The ingredients should be sufficient for two pans).  First, place spoonsful of tomato sauce on the bottom of the pan. Then, place a layer each of the following in order: pasta, sauce, meat mixture, spoonsful of ricotta, slices of mozzarella, grated cheese and meat mixture. Repeat layering beginning with sauce. Bake covered for approximately 30 minutes.

**Linguine with Olive Oil**

**1 lb. linguine**

**⅓ cup olive oil**

**4 cloves garlic**

**Parsley, chopped**

**Anchovies, chopped (optional)**

**Salt and pepper**

**Parmesan cheese, optional**

Brown garlic in oil. Set aside. Boil a large pot of water. When water has boiled, add the linguine to the water and cook until done to individual taste.

Drain linguine in a colander that is in a bowl, to preserve some of the pasta water. Return the linguine to the pot and pour the olive oil and garlic over the linguine. (You may want to remove the garlic, if so desired.) Add parsley. The amount is determined by preference.

Salt and pepper to taste. If linguine is too dry, add some of the pasta water. Serve with grated parmesan cheese. Also, I like to sprinkle red pepper onto my serving of linguine. But, this is a personal choice. Also, when adding the parsley, you may want to add anchovies, which gives a distinctly different taste to the pasta. Of course, you have to like anchovies.

## Linguine Primavera Salad

¼ cup olive oil

3 tablespoons fresh lemon juice

1 cup broccoli flowerets (1 inch long)

2 small zucchini trimmed, quartered lengthwise and cut crosswise into one-inch lengths.

4 asparagus spears, trimmed, cut into one-inch lengths

½ pound green beans, trimmed and cut into one-inch lengths.

1 tablespoon minced oregano or 1 teaspoon dried

½ pound fresh peas, shelled

3 tablespoons minced fresh thyme or 1 teaspoon dried

6 tablespoons olive oil

2 cups mushrooms, sliced thin

1 teaspoon red or green chili pepper, finely minced and seeded or ¼ teaspoon crushed dried red pepper

¼ cup, plus 2 tablespoons fresh minced parsley

2 teaspoons minced garlic

5 medium firm ripe tomatoes, peeled, cored and cut into one-inch cubes

¼ cup chopped fresh basil leaves (or 1 teaspoon dried basil), crumbled and chopped with 2 tablespoons parsley.

1 pound linguine

½ cup Parmesan cheese

**Salt and pepper to taste**

**1/3 cup toasted pine nuts.**


Prepare marinade by blending olive oil and lemon juice together. Set aside. Steam broccoli over boiling water, covered until crisp (3 minutes). Steam zucchini (two minutes). Steam asparagus (five minutes). Sprinkle green beans with oregano and steam until tender (eight minutes). Sprinkle peas with thyme and steam until peas are tender. Drain all vegetables and place in large bowl.

Heat one tablespoon olive oil in skillet. Add mushrooms, chili pepper and ¼ cup parsley. Sauté. Add vegetables. Set aside.

Heat 3 tablespoons olive oil in same skillet. Add garlic and tomatoes. Cook stirring gently. For five minutes. Stir in basil. Remove from heat. Reserve.

Heat remaining 2 tablespoons oil in clean skillet. Add and sauté garlic. Add vegetables. Sauté about two minutes. Transfer to large serving bowl. Cook linguine. Pour vinaigrette over vegetables in serving bowl. Toss to coat well. Marinate five minutes. Add tomato mixture, linguine, cheese, salt and pepper. Garnish with pine nuts and two tablespoons parsley. Serve at room temperature or refrigerate covered until cold.

**Spaghetti with White Clam Sauce**

This recipe comes from my book "Gioacchino: Memoir of an Italian Immigrant" about the life of the late Jack DiScala, a former real estate developer in Norwalk, Connecticut. The memoir includes a selection of DiScala family recipes.

**Sauce:**

**½ cup olive oil**

**4 cloves garlic, diced**

**1/3 cup clam juice**

**½ teaspoon dried oregano**

**Fresh ground pepper to taste**

**Salt**

**24 raw clams, minced**

**2 tablespoons parsley, chopped**

**Red pepper to taste**

**1 pound linguine**

In a medium skillet, heat the oil and sauté the garlic until it barely begins to color. Remove from the flame and let cool. Add the clam juice, oregano, ¼ teaspoon black pepper and ¼ teaspoon salt. Simmer for 5 minutes.

Add the minced clams with their juices, stirring well. Then cook, uncovered for 8 to 9 minutes, so that the liquid will reduce a bit. Stir in one tablespoon of the parsley and mix well.

Cook the spaghetti in 5 to 6 quarts of salted boiling water until al dente. Drain well and place in a large serving bowl. Add half the clam sauce; toss well, and then place the remaining clam sauce on top of the pasta and sprinkle the remaining parsley on top. If preferred, add more black pepper and hot pepper before serving.

**Rice Dishes**

My mother-in-law taught me how to cook two Pilaf (rice) dishes from Norman's mother. One is Pilaf made with rice and the other is a rice and orzo dish. Both rice dishes complement an entree, whether it is roast chicken, lamb or beef, which were Grandma's three favorite meats that she would often serve along with a green vegetable and a salad. If Grandma felt ambitious, she would also serve her own handmade stuffed grape leaves and boregs.

## Pilaf

**2 cups water**
**½ cup butter or margarine**
**3 tablespoons tomato sauce**
**Salt and pepper to taste**
**1 cup rice**

Boil first four ingredients Add 1 cup rice. Bring to a boil again Simmer until water is absorbed and rice is done.

## Pilaf (with orzo)

**¼ cup butter**

**1 cup orzo**

**1 cup rice**

**2 to 3 cups water**

**1 packet instant chicken broth or cubes.**

Brown orzo in butter in frying pan. Add rice. Stir. Add water and chicken broth packet (enough liquid to be one-inch above rice. Bring to a boil. Simmer until rice and orzo are done and water is absorbed.

# The Blue Zones' Recipe for Living Longer

The other day I told one of my grandsons that I wanted to live to be 100, and we figured out how old he would be when I reached that goal. My conversation with my grandson was spurred by a book I had just read, "The Blue Zones: Lessons for Living Longer from the People Who've Lived the Longest." First published in 2008, the book is the outgrowth of a magazine article, "The Secrets of Long Life," published in the November 2005 issue of "National Geographic." "Blue Zones" is a term coined by demographers while mapping one of these regions on the island of Sardinia.

In the magazine article, author Dan Buettner focused on three regions of the world in which research scientists, funded in part by the U.S. National Institute on Aging, studied people who live significantly longer – the majority were centenarians. These regions are Sardinia, Italy, Okinawa, Japan and Loma Linda, California, where the researchers studied a group of Seventh-Day Adventists who, Buettner wrote, ranked "among America's longevity all-stars."

Following the publication of the article, Buettner and a team of medical scientists, demographers and journalists traveled to five of the "healthiest corners of the globe," to report on the high rate of the longest-living people. In addition to Sardinia, Okinawa and Loma Linda, the book includes chapters on Nicoya, Costa Rica and Ikaria, a Greek island about 30 miles off the western coast of Turkey in the Aegean Sea.

Buettner writes in a very personable manner with a text not bogged down in scientific jargon, but in layman's terms. He brings the reader right into the home environment of the centenarians and we feel as if we are sharing a meal or sipping tea or a glass of wine right with him and his subjects at the table as the warm breezes blow into the room.

Okay, so here's the deal. Here's the not so magical formula or recipe for longevity. Yes, oh yes, it's diet and exercise, family, faith, friends, rest, low stress, and a purposeful life. Here's an interesting point noted in the book. There is a correlation between faith and longevity. One Costa Rican centenarian believed that "no matter how bad things got, God would take care of everything. This reliance on God becomes a stress-reliever.

"They tend to relinquish control of their lives to God. The fact that God is in control of their lives relieves any economic, spiritual or well-being anxiety they might otherwise have. Someone is looking out for them," Buettner says. The author notes that the Seventh-Day Adventist faith was rooted in a strong faith tradition; Okinawan elders believed that their deceased ancestors watched over them; and Sardinians were devout Catholics.

In his magazine article, Buettner presents a graphic illustrating how "seniors in three widely separated regions — Sardinia, Loma Linda and Okinawa, share a number of key habits, despite many differences in backgrounds and beliefs. In each Blue Zone, the elders do not smoke; they put family first; they are active every day; they keep socially engaged; they eat fruits, vegetables and whole grains. In addition, the Sardinians drink red wine and eat Pecorino cheese. The Adventists eat nuts and beans and the Okinawans eat small portions.

Buettner notes that in the U.S., the rate of female to male centenarians is about four to one. In parts of Sardinia, it's more like one-to-one.  Also, he notes Okinawans have fewer heart attacks than their U.S. counterparts and lower rates of breast and prostate cancer.

In the book, Buettner notes a characteristic of longevity among the centenarians in Ikaria. They like their naps. Buettner writes, "The bottom line: Your kindergarten teacher may have had it right." The Ikarians take a mid-afternoon break. "People, he says, "who nap regularly have up to 35 percent lower chances of dying from heart disease...napping lowers stress hormones or rests the heart."

Another interesting point I came away with in reading the book is that while many of the older people studied lived long lives, their lives may not have been necessarily void of disease or illness. However, their healthy lifestyles helped in coping with their health problems and in certain cases, avoiding death from the health affliction.

Other interesting observations: honey may help control blood sugar levels; darker honey has more antioxidants and less water than lighter honey. Oranges, a source of Vitamin C, fiber and potassium help prevent heart disease, cancer and stroke.  Also, sleep is important in keeping the immune system functioning, reduces risk of heart attack and recharges the brain.  Buettner advises seven to nine hours of sleep a night; go to bed the same time and get up the same time. Sleep in a dark, quiet cool room and on a comfortable mattress and pillow.

The best part of this book is Buettner's explaining how each of us can create our own "Blue Zone" in our own life. He offers the "Power Nine" lessons patterned after the lifestyles of the Blue Zones centenarians but modified to fit the Western lifestyle.

I am determined to create my own "Blue Zone." I want to see my grandchildren graduate college, get married if they so desire; and live purposeful lives. I want to see my great-grandchildren.

I don't want my life patterned after the final year of my father's life struggling with colon cancer that took his life. As he struggled with the disease at age 61, he lamented that it must have been caused by "all the steak I ate." The Centenarians in the Blue Zones would surely agree.

# Meat

## Beef with Vegetables

**1 ½ pounds beef sirloin or tenderloin, ½ to ¾ inch thick**

**1 garlic clove, minced**

**½ cup water**

**⅓ cup soy sauce**

**¼ cup cooking oil**

**1 green pepper, cleaned and cut into thin slices, lengthwise.**

**1 cup thinly sliced celery**

**2 medium onions, thinly sliced**

**2 cups thinly sliced cabbage**

**2 cans (6 ounces) water chestnuts, drained**

**2 cans (4 ounces) sliced mushrooms, drained**

**½ tablespoon cornstarch**

**1 can (8 ounces) tomato juice**

Chill meat in freezer until partially frozen. This makes slicing easier. Cut meat across the grain into very thin pieces. Place meat in bowl. Combine garlic, water and soy sauce. Pour over meat and mix. Cover. Refrigerate 45 minutes to one hour. Drain meat. Save marinade. Pat meat dry on paper towel. Heat oil in wok or frying pan.

Brown meat quickly, stirring constantly. Add onion, pepper, celery, cabbage, water chestnuts and mushrooms. Stir and fry just until vegetables are tender, yet crisp — 3 to 4 minutes. Combine cornstarch, remaining marinade and tomato juice. Stir until smooth, and add to vegetables. Stir until mixture thickens.

Serve with fluffy white rice. Serve with a vegetable side dish such as carrots or zucchini. (Diagonally cut the vegetables and fry in oil. Season with chicken broth. Cook until crisp and tender).

## Braciole

My mother would add meat to her tomato sauce while it was cooking. She would choose from a variety of meats, often selecting a beef and pork to flavor the sauce. The beef would be meatballs or braciole, which is a piece of round steak. The pork would be either sweet and/or hot Italian sausage or spareribs. Each meat or combination of meats offers a variety of flavors to the sauce.

**1 ½ pounds round steak cut into 9-inch slices**

**2 tablespoons grated parmesan cheese**

**1 clove garlic**

**½ tablespoon salt**

**Pepper**

**1 teaspoon chopped parsley**

**2 tablespoons olive oil**

**2 slices of bacon, uncooked**

Place meat on a board. Combine cheese, garlic, salt, pepper, parsley and oil to form a paste. Spread mixture onto meat slices. Top with bacon. Roll up slices and tie with soft string. Brown rolled meat in hot olive oil. Place in tomato sauce. When ready to serve dinner, remove braciole from the sauce and cool. Slice meat crosswise into 3/4 inch pieces. Top with sauce and serve with pasta.

## Cha Shui (Pork Tenderloins)

**2 pork tenderloins**

**1 cup soy sauce**

**¼ to 1 cup brown sugar**

**1 teaspoon fresh ginger root**

**3 cloves garlic crushed**

**⅓ cup sherry**

Preheat oven to 350 degrees

Marinate meat for four hours. Massage meat three minutes. Bake for ¼ to one hour. Turn frequently to brown all sides. Cool meat. Cut into thin diagonal slices. Serve with soy sauce, Chinese mustard, or sweet and sour sauce.

## Cold Braised Beef

This is a great dish to serve guests, especially in the summer time. It seems as if every time I serve it to a new guest, I receive a lot of compliments and requests for the recipe. I have to give credit to my friend Pam Schaeffer, a former neighbor in St. Louis, Missouri, who served this roast beef when I had dinner at her house in the late 1960s. Fortunately, I had asked for the recipe and have been serving it for the past 45 years. In the summer, I like to complement this meat dish with my cole slaw recipe, which I also credit my stay in St. Louis. The cole slaw recipe, which is included in this book in the salad section, came from a small spiral-bound cookbook compiled by the PTA at the Henry Avenue Elementary School in Ballwin, Missouri, where my daughter Maria attended Kindergarten before the family moved to Connecticut in 1971.

The key to serving a successful platter of marinated cold roast beef is to have the meat sliced at the deli counter the day of

preparing the dish or no earlier than the day before serving.
Sliced roast beef tastes best when served soon after purchase.

**3 tablespoons red wine vinegar**

**1 teaspoon salt and pepper**

**1 teaspoon dry mustard**

**9 tablespoons olive oil**

**2 tablespoons capers in salt — rinse off salt thoroughly;
coarsely chopped**

**½ teaspoon garlic, finely chopped**

**2-3 tablespoons parsley**

**½ cup onion, thinly sliced**

**12 slices roast beef, (one pound) cut thinly**

Prepare two to three hours before serving. Make marinade by
combining vinegar, salt, pepper and mustard. Mix to dissolve. Beat
in olive oil. Add capers, garlic and parsley. Set aside. Layer slices
of meat, one slice at a time, in a shallow oblong glass baking dish.
Scatter onions on top of meat between layers. Spread marinade
over each slice. Repeat process. Add additional parsley and serve.

## Hawaiian Casserole

1 ½ pounds ground beef

½ pound pork

1 teaspoon salt

2 tablespoons oil

1 cup chicken bouillon

¾ cup pineapple tidbits

12 Maraschino cherries

1 green pepper, cut in rings

3 tablespoons cornstarch

½ cup light corn syrup

1 tablespoon soy sauce

2 tablespoons vinegar

Preheat oven to 300 degrees

Combine first three ingredients. Brown in oil. Add bouillon and simmer. Add next three ingredients. Simmer for 15 minutes covered. Combine remaining ingredients. Place with other ingredients in casserole. Bake for 15 minutes.

## Chili

**1 lb. ground beef**

**1 can red kidney beans**

**1 can pork and beans**

**2 tsp. chili powder**

**2 onions**

**1 can tomatoes.**

Brown ground beef. Add remaining ingredients to beef. Simmer

## Flank Steak

**½ cup oil**

**2 tablespoons lemon juice**

**½ teaspoon garlic powder**

**1 teaspoon onion salt**

**½ teaspoon pepper**

**½ teaspoon salt**

**1 teaspoon Worcestershire sauce**

**Flank Steak**

Combine first seven ingredients to make marinade. Then, marinate steak for six hours at room temperature. Turn occasionally. Broil five minutes on each side. Baste frequently with marinade. Carve into thin slices.

## Hamburger Quiche

1 unbaked 9-inch pastry shell

½ pound ground beef

1 ½ cup mayonnaise

½ cup milk

2 eggs

1 tablespoon cornstarch

1 ½ lbs. cheddar or Swiss cheese

⅓ cup sliced green onion

Dash of pepper

Preheat oven to 350 degrees

Brown meat in skillet over medium heat. Drain fat and set aside. Blend next four ingredients until smooth. Stir in meat, cheese, onion and pepper. Turn into pastry shell. Bake for 35 to 40 minutes or until golden brown on top and knife inserted in center comes out clean. Serves six to eight.


## Hot Franks with Devil Dip

1 package frankfurters

1 tablespoon vegetable oil

¼ cup finely chopped onion

1 8-ounce can tomato sauce with cheese

1 tablespoon prepared mustard

**Dash Tabasco sauce**

Slice frankfurters into one-inch chunks. Brown in oil in skillet. Stick with toothpicks for serving Serve with the dipping sauce made from tomato sauce with cheese, onion, mustard and Tabasco, combined and simmered in saucepan for five minutes. Makes about 30 hot dog snacks.

**Meatballs**

Note: I found a lined yellow piece of paper among my mother's recipe index cards. In her handwriting my mother wrote "Mary's Recipes" which in addition to this meatballs recipe included a recipe for marinated chicken and for tomato sauce. My Aunt Mary was a wonderful cook.

While this recipe calls for beef or all veal, I realize that through the years, I have made meatballs with three kinds of meat: ground beef, veal and pork. Experiment. Use one kind of meat, two or all three in equal parts. I also add chopped onion and sometimes I will use one cup bread crumbs instead of the bread. I've noticed that in perusing cookbooks some recipes call for coating meatballs with flour before frying in oil.

**1 pound chopped beef or all veal**

**6 slices bread, soaked thoroughly**

**2 eggs**

**Garlic, one clove, chopped very fine**

**Parsley, chopped, fine**

**½ cup Parmesan cheese**

**Oil for frying**

After a good soaking, remove the crust from the bread. Combine the meat, bread, eggs, garlic, parsley and cheese.  Form into balls and fry in oil.


**Bernice's Meat Loaf**


**2 cups bread crumbs (or break up fresh bread)**

**¾ cup minced onion**

**¼ cup minced green pepper**

**2 eggs, lightly beaten**

**2 pounds ground chuck beef**

**2 tablespoons horseradish**

**2 ½ teaspoons salt**

**2 ½ teaspoons dry mustard**

**¼ cup milk**

**¾ cup ketchup, ¼ mixed in meat, ½ spread on top of meatloaf**


Preheat oven to 400 degrees.

Mix all ingredients and place in pan. (Shallow pan for firmness or loaf pan for a soft moist texture). Bake for 50 minutes.


**Round Steak with Beer and Tomato**


**2 pounds round steak**

**Salt and pepper**

**1 onion**

**1 can (14 oz.) tomatoes**

**½ teaspoon oregano**

**¼ teaspoon basil**

**1 teaspoon Worcestershire sauce**

**¾ cup beer**

Preheat oven to 350 degrees

Pound flour into round steak. Cut meat into serving pieces. Salt and pepper meat. Brown in oil. Place in casserole. Sauté onions in oil. Add remaining ingredients. Bring to a boil. Pour over meat. Bake for one and one-half hours.

## Italian Sausage Pie

**1 package pie crust mix**

**½ teaspoon baking powder**

**½ beaten egg (save other half)**

**½ teaspoon white vinegar**

**¼ cup cold water**

**1 pound Italian sausage**

**4 eggs**

**½ cup Italian grating cheese**

**2 tablespoons chopped parsley**

**Salt and pepper**

Preheat oven to 350 degrees

Combine pie crust mix and baking powder; add next three ingredients and mix quickly with fork until dough is formed. Wrap dough in wax paper and set aside. Remove sausage from casing and fry slowly until cooked. Drain and cool, reserving one tablespoon fat from the pan. Beat eggs, including the saved ½ egg from the crust with the cheese, parsley, salt and pepper. Add sausage to the egg mixture with the fat. Mix together, and let stand while rolling crust. This helps to thicken the mixture slightly. Divide dough; roll to fit bottom and top of 9-inch pie pan. Place dough in bottom; pour in sausage mixture; place top with ventilation slits and brush with egg yolk and water for a glazed crust. Bake for 30 minutes or until well- browned. May be served hot or cold.

**Teriyaki (sirloin or chicken)**

**1 pound beef or chicken**

**2 teaspoons ginger**

**2 garlic cloves, chopped**

**4 ounces onion**

**4 teaspoons sugar**

**½ cup soy sauce**

**¼ cup water**

Marinate meat in combined ingredients for one or two hours. Broil.

## Veal Marsala

1 garlic clove

2 pounds veal cut in 2- inch squares

Flour

Salt and pepper

Olive oil

½ cup Marsala wine

Parsley, fresh, chopped

Coat veal slices with flour, salt and pepper. Brown veal in oil. While veal is browning, combine wine, ½ cup water, parsley and salt and pepper (to taste). When veal is browned, add wine mixture and slowly simmer for about 20 minutes or until veal is tender. If mixture becomes too thick, add a small amount of water.

## Veal Paprika

1 ½ pounds veal, sliced into small pieces

1 tablespoon shortening

½ teaspoon paprika

¼ teaspoon black pepper

1 teaspoon salt

1 onion, chopped

1 tablespoon parsley

½ pound mushrooms

**½ pint sour cream**

**1 tablespoon flour**

Melt shortening. Add onion, paprika, pepper, salt, and parsley. Add meat. Cover and cook for one hour. Add mushrooms and cook until tender. Add the flour. Blend well and cook for five minutes. Add sour cream. Serve with rice or mashed potatoes.

**Veal Scaloppini**

**1 pound veal cutlets**

**Flour**

**6 tablespoons butter**

**Salt and pepper**

**¼ cup sherry**

**2 tablespoons parsley, chopped**

**½ can mushrooms, sliced**

Veal should be sliced thin and pounded with a mallet. Dip veal cutlet into flour. Sauté in butter in large skillet for 3 to 4 minutes on each side. Sprinkle with salt and pepper. Add sherry. Add parsley and mushrooms. Simmer for 10 minutes more. Serves four.

# DiSpirito: The Good Life Comes with Food, Family, Friends

Pssst! Do you have five minutes? That's all you'll need if you're cooking with Rocco DiSpirito.

This celebrity cook, ex-restaurant owner and one-time reality show star of "The Restaurant" stopped in Madison, Connecticut, in 2005 to promote his cookbook, "Rocco's 5 Minute Flavor" at the Scranton Memorial Library.

Rocco was accompanied by his mother Nicolina DiSpirito, who is just as much a crowd pleaser as her good-looking, charming chef-son. But, it's Rocco's third cookbook that will charm the apron off any cook.

His cookbook offers 175 recipes made with five ingredients and cooked in five minutes (not counting shopping or prep time) at no more than five dollars a serving. The recipes range from appetizers, fondues, soups, salads and sandwiches to sides, main dishes and desserts.

In writing this cookbook, it is Rocco's intentions that people indeed will "Grab the good life." Rocco explained his signature phrase.

"The good life is the energy among people. It's about people enjoying the energy of others." He said that it's ironic that because of his profession people would think the good life would mean eating *fois gras* pate, a Kobe steak, or fresh scallops from Maine.

"It turns out those things are secondary and tertiary. Those are the facilitators, the devices we use to help feel the good life. This is something I learned from my family that is very valuable. Regardless of socioeconomic status, education, where you live, what you have, what you own, what you don't own, what people think about you, the good life is yours for the taking...Ultimately, it's the energy of others; it's enjoying the energy of other people, and food is usually one of the ways we do that.

"We sit around a table that is round on purpose. You face people; you look into their eyes and often the good life is around a dinner table. Certainly, I've experienced that."

With "Rocco's 5 Minute Flavor" cookbook, people can cook and eat well without spending a lot of time in the kitchen.

"Supermarkets and grocery stores have responded to Americans who want to eat better, but don't have time. So they are now offering more and more prepared foods, frozen foods, condiments, completely cooked foods, heat n' eat foods, microwavable foods that are getting better and better...This cookbook comes from my getting out of the restaurants and cooking at home – taking for granted that I knew what I would be doing at home because I knew what I was doing in a restaurant.

"It turns out that wasn't the case at all. Cooking at home is very different. You don't have the time. You don't have the help and you don't have the money. So, somehow because of my knowledge and skills of food, I was able to shop strategically and still put food together very, very quickly. For me home-cooking for myself or for friends is often a can of black beans, a grilled piece of salmon, some sherry vinegar and some chopped scallions and a square dish."

In researching the book, Rocco became a personal shopper. He went into grocery stores and selected several hundred (he included a hundred in the book) prepared high quality short-cut foods and incorporated them with fresh foods that are also sold in such a way that you can cook them quickly, such as chicken breast versus thin sliced chicken cutlets.

"It's an obvious choice when you're thinking about speed," Rocco said "Chicken cutlets cook almost instantly. Chicken breasts take 30 minutes."

One of Rocco's favorite recipes in his cookbook is "Pretzelized Chicken with Cheddar Horseradish Sauce." Here, chicken cutlets are seasoned with salt and pepper, dipped into egg and then dredged in pretzel crumbs and fried in oil. The chicken is served on a bed of spinach that has been cooked in oil. The chicken is topped with a horseradish cheese sauce.

In his book, Rocco lists five pantry ingredients every cook should have: salt and pepper, sugar, vinegar, fat and flour. Also, he lists five pieces of kitchen equipment to cook every recipe in the cookbook: a sauté pan, a stovetop grill pan, a six-to-eight quart stockpot or pasta pot, a broiler and a microwave oven. In addition, he lists 100 high quality prepared food ingredients that are used in the book. These range from mashed potatoes and spicy brown mustard to Thai sauce.

He said the international aisle in a supermarket is a "gold mine of flavor. There are flavor detonators in cans and in jars; things that will help you rocket your food to the flavor stratosphere.

"It's not just macaroni and cheese here. My dishes are about giant flavor combinations. Very exciting explosions in the mouth."

Former owner of Manhattan's Union Pacific and Rocco's restaurants, Rocco loves the restaurant world because he gets to interact with people. That interaction has been evident to anyone who has listened to his former radio program, "Food Talk," on WOR.

"When people talk about food and wine and drink and partying, they are always happy. There's always a sparkle in their eyes," said Rocco, explaining the enthusiasm of his radio listeners.

"I heard this from people who say, 'I can hear the smile in your voice on the radio.' Apparently, that is the greatest compliment you can get on the radio. I feel I really help them without intimidating them. I'm trying to empower them to do things they didn't think they could do."

In introducing Rocco, Roxanne Coady, owner of R.J. Julia Booksellers, who sponsored his talk, said the cookbook author has the interesting combination of having gone to the Culinary Institute of America and to business school. He earned a business degree from Boston University in 1989.

Coady said, "If you have the pantry stocked the way Rocco tells you to have it in this book and someone calls up last minute for dinner, you can have them over for dinner."

Rocco, who returned to Madison for his third appearance said, "For a city boy, (he grew up in Jamaica, Queens) it's nice to know I have a home in Madison, Connecticut.

The son of Italian immigrants, Rocco was always curious as a child, especially about food. He thought "some kind of magic happened in the kitchen. As the youngest in the family, he was very close to his mother and especially to his grandmother.
"My grandmother lived a very Italian lifestyle. She had a chicken coop, the wine; she did that whole thing. For me they were some kind of magicians. They were like gods to me. I was drawn to my mother and because she spent a lot of time in the kitchen cooking it became part of what I enjoyed about her. When it came time for my first job, as a result of my asking for an allowance increase,"

she said, 'Well, if you want an allowance increase, go get a job.' So I said, 'Okay, I'll do that' and it seemed natural that I would go to a restaurant. And I was immediately struck by the interaction of people—the energy of other people and the dichotomy of the test of discipline and creative freedom on a level that I hadn't felt in my life yet.

"The kitchen is an interesting place that way. Restaurants are interesting that way. They require a military discipline, yet at the same time there's so much room for what's in your heart."

# Poultry

## Skinny Shake — Coating for Chicken or Fish

**Fish fillets**

**Chicken pieces**

**4 cups unseasoned breadcrumbs**

**1 teaspoon salt**

**1 teaspoon paprika**

**1 teaspoon celery salt**

**1 teaspoon pepper**

**½ cup vegetable oil**

Mix ingredients together and coat fish or chicken. Ingredients are enough for 30 servings of fish or 20 pieces of chicken.


**Marinade for Chicken**

**1 can frozen lemonade**

**3 tablespoons lime juice**

**2 teaspoons bitters**

**¼ pound butter**

**1 three pound chicken or chicken parts**

Defrost frozen lemonade and mix with ingredients. Coat chicken with marinade. Chill for a few hours and barbecue or roast in oven.

## Barbecue Chicken

1 whole chicken cut up

½ teaspoon pepper

½ teaspoon paprika

½ teaspoon salt

1 teaspoon dry mustard

1 small onion chopped

1 tablespoon brown sugar

2 teaspoons Worcestershire sauce

1 teaspoon Tabasco sauce

1 garlic clove, chopped

½ cup red wine vinegar

¼ cup vegetable oil

½ cup tomato juice

Preheat oven to 325 degrees

Place chicken in shallow oven dish. Combine remaining ingredients in a saucepan and simmer for a few minutes. Pour over chicken. Bake for one and one-half hours, turning and basting every half hour.

## Chicken a la King

¼ cup melted butter or margarine

3 tablespoons flour

1 cup chicken broth

1 cup milk.

1 teaspoon salt

2 cups diced cooked chicken

1 3-ounce can of sliced mushrooms, drained and broiled

¼ cup chopped pimento

Blend butter or margarine with flour. Blend in chicken broth and milk. Cook stirring constantly over low heat until sauce is thick. Add salt, chicken, mushrooms and pimento. Heat through. Serve over hot toast points.

## Chicken Breasts

3 large chicken breasts, cut in halves

Salt and pepper

1 chicken bouillon cube

¼ cup dry white wine

½ teaspoon instant minced onions

¼ teaspoon curry powder

2 tablespoons flour

**Water**

**1 3-ounce can sliced mushrooms, drained**

**Watercress**

Preheat oven to 350 degrees

Place chicken breasts in 12x7"x2" baking dish. Salt and add a dash of paprika. Dissolve bouillon cube in 1 cup boiling water. Add wine, onions, curry powder and dash of pepper. Pour over chicken. Cover with foil. Bake for 30 minutes. Uncover and bake an additional 45 minutes or until tender. Remove chicken to warm serving platter.

Strain pan juices. Reserve juice for sauce made by blending 2 tablespoons flour and ¼ cup cold water in saucepan. Slowly stir in pan juices. Cook and stir over low heat until sauce thickens. Boil and stir 3 to 4 minutes. Add mushrooms. Heat through. Spoon over chicken breasts. Garnish with watercress.

## Chicken Casserole

**3 tablespoons butter**

**3 tablespoons flour**

**1 ½ cups chicken broth or 2 chicken bouillons in 1 ½ cups water**

**2 cups cooked chicken cut into pieces**

**1 cup drained cooked peas**

**1 3 ounce can sliced mushroom, drained**

**1 carrot, cooked and cut in fourths**

**¼ cup chopped onion**

**2 tablespoons chopped pimento**

**½ teaspoon salt**

**1 package refrigerated biscuits**

Preheat oven to 425 degrees

Melt butter. Blend in flour. Gradually add broth. Cook and stir until thick. Add chicken, vegetables, salt. Pour into 1 ½ quart casserole dish. Cut six biscuits in quarters and arrange around edge of casserole. Bake for 8 to 10 minutes.

## Chicken Chow Mein

**6 to 8 onion rings**

**½ pound margarine**

**1 celery rib, cubed**

**1 to 2 cups chicken broth**

**2 cans bean sprouts, rinsed**

**Water chestnuts, sliced**

**Cooked chicken, cubed**

**2 tablespoons cornstarch**

**Soy sauce**

**3 cups cooked rice**

Sauté onion in margarine. Add celery and 1 cup chicken broth. Cook until tender. Add bean sprouts and water chestnuts. Add chicken and additional chicken broth. Mix cornstarch, water and soy sauce. Add to hot chow mein. Add salt and pepper. Put over three cups cooked rice. Serves six.

## Chicken Cutlets Marsala

**6 chicken cutlets**

**Flour**

**¼ teaspoon salt**

**½ teaspoon paprika**

**1 pound mushrooms**

**1 cup chicken broth**

**Marsala wine**

Preheat oven to 350 degrees

Dip chicken in flour, salt and paprika. Sauté. Place chicken in shallow pan. Steam mushrooms. Add with liquid to pan. Add chicken broth. Bake for 35 minutes. Last five minutes add Marsala.

## Chicken Divan

**3 chicken breasts cooked and thinly sliced**

**2 bunches broccoli or one 10-ounce package frozen**

**¼ cup butter or margarine**

**¼ cup flour**

**2 cups chicken broth**

½ cup whipping cream

3 tablespoons cooking sherry

½ teaspoon salt

¼ cup Parmesan cheese


Preheat oven to 350 degrees

Cook broccoli. Drain. Melt butter and blend in flour. Add chicken broth. Cook and stir until thick. Stir in cream, sherry, salt and a dash of pepper. Place broccoli crosswise in 13"x 9"x 2" baking dish. Pour half the sauce over the broccoli. Top with chicken slices. To remaining sauce, add Parmesan cheese. Pour over chicken. Sprinkle with extra parmesan cheese. Bake for 20 minutes or until hot through. Broil until sauce is golden.


**Chicken Piccata**


**3 whole chicken breasts, boned, skinned and halved (chicken tenders can be used instead of breasts)**

**1 egg, beaten with one tablespoon water**

**½ cup breadcrumbs**

**½ cup Parmesan and/or Romano cheese**

**2 tablespoons olive oil**

**1 ½ cups chicken broth**

**2 tablespoons all-purpose flour**

**¼ cup lemon juice**

**¼ cup Italian parsley**

**2-3 tablespoons capers, optional**

Dip chicken into egg and then into a mixture of breadcrumbs and cheese. Brown chicken on both sides in a skillet with oil. Blend flour and lemon juice and then stir into skillet. Cook, stirring until thickened and smooth. Add parsley. Serve over cooked pasta, such as spaghetti or linguine.

**Marinated Chicken**

**4 tablespoons soy sauce**

**½ lemon, squeezed**

**Parsley, chopped**

**Garlic clove, quartered**

**2 tablespoons vegetable oil**

**6 pieces of chicken**

Preheat oven to 350 degrees

Combine the first five ingredients. Pour over chicken and marinate for a few hours. Bake until chicken is tender.

**Baked Chicken Parmesan**

**½ cup salad oil**

**2 broiler-fryer chicken cut into serving pieces**

**1 ½ teaspoon oregano, divided**

**1 ½ teaspoons salt, divided**

**Paprika**

**2 cans (3 or 4 ounces each) sliced mushrooms**

**4 tablespoons grated Parmesan cheese**

Preheat oven to 425 degrees.

Line a 15" by 10" by 1-inch shallow baking pan with aluminum foil. Pour salad oil into pan. Place in oven to heat about 10 minutes. Remove pan from oven. Place chicken pieces, skin side down, in hot oil. Sprinkle with half the oregano and salt. Sprinkle lightly with paprika. Return to oven and bake 30 minutes. Turn chicken pieces.

Sprinkle with remaining oregano, salt and paprika. Bake 15 minutes longer. Remove from oven. Spoon fat and drippings in pan over chicken. Pour mushrooms with liquid over chicken. Sprinkle with grated Parmesan cheese. Bake 5 minutes longer. Serves 12.

# Rachael Ray: a Multimedia Success Story in Food Industry

As a child it would not be uncommon for Rachael Ray to bring to school a lunch sandwich with anchovies and provolone on Italian bread. After all, she said, in a telephone interview, she had the "diet of a 75-year-old man."

Why was that?

Ray, whose natural talents have catapulted her into one of America's favorite television personalities, celebrity chefs and cookbook authors, grew up in an upstate New York household where her Sicilian grandfather, a fixture in the kitchen with his love of cooking and food, was a driving force in the Scuderi/Ray household.

Ray's grandfather's love of cooking was passed down to his daughter Elsa, Ray's mother, the oldest of ten children. She has enjoyed her own career in the food industry, managing four restaurants on Cape Cod among other restaurant positions. Rachael's own building-block career spans from her candy counter post at Macy's to a best-selling cookbook author, award-winning TV host and philanthropist who founded the nonprofit organization Yum-O! to empower children and their families to develop healthy relationships with food and cooking. This is achieved by teaching families to cook, feeding hungry kids and funding cooking education.

Ray's success in the food entertainment industry in less than a decade demonstrates what one can accomplish with the natural talents, passion and energy. She has managed to combine her anti-Martha Stewart lifestyle with what "Vanity Fair" has dubbed her Sophia Loren's little sister charm into a multi-million dollar industry generated through the sale of her cookbooks and the popularity of her TV shows that along with her shows " Tasty Travels" and" Rachael's Vacation." She is also founder and editorial director of her magazine, "Every day with Rachael Ray."

Not only is Rachael Ray a multimedia success story, in 2010 she expanded her publishing empire with her 17th cookbook, Rachael Ray's "Look Cook" (Clarkson Potter/Publishers) into the realm of multimedia. The cookbook offers never-before published recipes, and 600-four-color photographs. The first 170 recipes are each accompanied by up to eight step-by-step instructive color photographs. Additionally, Ray demonstrates recipes in online videos, hosted on FoodNetwork.com and RachaelRay.com. The purpose is to visually demonstrate the simplicity in the easy-step recipes at a moment's glance.

During the interview Ray explained that the cookbook's multimedia approach's purpose is to reflect the multimedia trends this country is adopting in the publishing industry. "How many people are downloading into gadgets today?" she said rhetorically. "It's great straight content with no commercials. It's the cooking equivalent to paint by numbers." Ray is fascinated by the added dimension that her latest cookbook offers.

"Rachael Ray's "Look + Cook" is divided into sections, reflecting Ray's familiar cooking and recipe style: Cozy Food; Make Your Own Takeout; Fancy Fake-Outs; 30-Minute Meals; Yes! The Kids will Eat It; Sides & Starters; Simple Sauces & Bottom-of-the-Jar Tips; and Desserts.

Ray explained the Takeout section offers the familiar and popular takeout-style foods that people love, but by offering these recipes that people can do in their own kitchen, they get to control the salt, fat and quantity. Also, she noted, that popular takeout-food establishments may not be available in many neighborhoods.

"We don't have takeout in the Adirondacks," said Ray, a reference to the scenic upstate New York area where she and her husband, have a home in the classic Adirondack Mountains cabin-style. She has been married since 2005 to John Cusimano, a lawyer who heads Ray's production company, Watch Entertainment and handles all her legal matters.

When made at home, takeout is "less of a guilty pleasure," says Ray, who invites readers to make their own takeout "and save on the tip."

In addition to the takeout meals, Ray selected the new cookbook's recipes to represent a cross-section of culinary tastes including a variety of "meatless meals, comfort food and bistro meals," she said. In addition, the cookbook's "Bottom of the Jar Tips," section is pure Ray creativity. For example, take the last few tablespoons of peanut butter sitting in the bottom of the jar and turn it into a spicy Thai peanut sauce as a dip for chicken tenders or pour over a pound of warm whole-wheat noodles and garnish with toasted sesame seeds and chopped scallions. She suggests: "loosen the peanut butter in the jar by microwaving it, with the lid off, for 30 seconds on high. Add three tablespoons of hot water and three tablespoons tamari, lime zest and juice from one lemon and one teaspoon of red pepper flakes to the jar. Screw the lid on and shake to combine.

While one may wonder where she gets all her ideas for her cookbooks and television shows, Ray offered a little peek in her life. She keeps a notebook, sometimes two at a time, and as she goes about her daily routines, she gathers ideas and jots them down in her notebooks with references to which future book project or TV show, cooking, lifestyle or travel, the idea would be appropriate. She loves to drop by newsstands and bookstores to peruse the latest magazines or look at old cookbooks at one of her favorite haunts, the "Strand" bookstore which is in her neighborhood where she lives with her husband, whom she met at a party. In past interviews, she has described their meeting. They were the two shortest people in the room and therefore, they gravitated to one another. Both recalled knowing that night that they had met their future mates. In a "Vanity Fair" interview, Ray's friend Donna Carnevale is quoted as saying," She said she was going to marry that man; she was going to marry him in Rome." They married in Montalcino, Italy in September 2005.

While Ray describes her notebook entries of ideas as a base for many of her projects, her habit of idea collecting can be traced back to her childhood when she spent many hours with paper and crayons. A chronic croup condition at as a child required her to spend many days in bed beneath a tent to relieve her congestion. She whiled the time away by drawing.

"I loved being home sick. Mom built the vaporizing tent," Ray says.

Keeping records of ideas is her "nervous energy thing," says Ray, who also noted that her husband, who loves to write songs, is always "writing down songs."

During the interview Ray harkened back to her childhood and the influence her family, especially her mother and grandfather have had on her strong love for working in the food industry. When the family moved back upstate from Cape Cod and her mother had other restaurant management jobs, Ray would spend time at her mother's work, watching and building her love for the food industry. She talks about how comforting it always has been for her and her family to be together cooking in the kitchen.

"It was a multi-generational household," said Ray, whose sparked her own early success when she worked in a local food market and decided to conduct food demonstrations so that shoppers would buy certain products. The demonstrations evolved into her concept of "30-Minute Meals" which led to a food demonstration segment on a local upstate television station. Eventually, when the "Today" show was looking for a last-minute replacement for a food segment, they called Ray. Her mother answered the telephone and it took a little convincing that it actually was the "Today" show calling. There was one drawback. New York was experiencing a blizzard-conditions snowstorm. A four-hour car trip took nine hours. However, her national broadcast proved a success. Also, at the same time the Food Network heard about Ray and contacted Ray.

According to the "Vanity Fair" interview in 2007, Ray said she told the Food Network, "Listen, you're champagne' I'm beer out of the bottle. I clearly don't belong here. I'm not a chef..." However, that was what the Food Network liked about Ray and obviously so do millions of viewers. She is the daughter, the sister, the neighbor next-door.

Not only is her personality what viewers like, her style of cooking is appealing as well. Who has time nowadays? Her" 30-Minute Meals" is just what people want and she has capitalized on that success again and again.

Through her nonprofit Yum-O! Ray works to empower young people to pay more attention to their food and also to work towards providing for themselves. One of her priorities is to see a "return to the lunchroom cook" in schools so that children will be served nutritional foods. Through lobbying she has been encouraging legislators to make a social change so that children eat better and as a result are better prepared to learn.

# Fish

## Baccala

**2 pounds cod or other thick fish**

**2 ½ teaspoons salt**

**⅛ teaspoon pepper**

**3 cups thinly sliced potatoes**

**3 cups thinly sliced onions**

**1 clove garlic minced**

**2 tablespoons olive oil**

**2 green peppers cut into rings**

**2 tomatoes cut into slices**

**2 bay leaves**

Preheat oven to 350 degrees.

Cut cod into large chunks. Combine salt and pepper. Add potatoes to large pot of rapidly boiling water Bring to a rapid boil again. Drain at once. Cook onion and garlic in oil and butter until onion is just limp. Layer onion mixture, sliced potatoes, green pepper rings, fish and tomato into shallow two quart baking dish. Sprinkle each layer with salt mixture. Add bay leaf. Cover with foil. Bake for one hour.

## Salmon Loaf

**1 pound can salmon**

**1 tablespoon lemon juice**

**Dash of cayenne**

152

1 teaspoon salt

2 eggs beaten

⅔ cup chopped celery

1 ½ cups breadcrumbs

½ teaspoon baking powder

½ cup evaporated milk

½ cup fish juice and water

Preheat oven to 350 degrees

Drain salmon. Discard skin and bones. Save juice. Flake fish. Add remaining ingredients. Mix well. Pack mixture firmly into a greased glass loaf pan. Bake until brown and firm. Approximately 30 to 40 minutes.

**Shrimp Creole**

1 large onion, sliced

2-3 stalks celery, chopped

2 tablespoons bacon fat

1 tablespoon flour

½ teaspoon salt

½ teaspoon pepper

1 teaspoon chili powder

1 cup water

1 (14 oz.) can crushed tomatoes

1 (6 oz.) can peas

**1 tablespoon vinegar**

**1 teaspoon sugar**

**1 pound cooked shrimp**

Brown onions and celery in bacon fat.  Blend in flour and seasonings. Add water. Stir slowly and constantly. Simmer for ten minutes covered. Add remaining ingredients and continue cooking for another 15 minutes until shrimp is thoroughly heated. Serve over cooked rice.

## Shrimp DeJonghe

**1 cup butter, melted**

**2 cloves garlic, minced**

**⅓ cup chopped parsley**

**½ teaspoon paprika**

**Dash of cayenne**

**⅔ cup cooking sherry**

**2 cups soft breadcrumbs**

**5 to 6 cups cleaned cooked shrimp (4 pounds in a shell)**

Preheat oven to 325 degrees

To melted butter, add next five ingredients. Mix. Add bread crumbs. Toss. Place shrimp in an 11"x7"x1 ½" baking dish. Spoon the butter mixture over the shrimp.  Bake in oven until crumbs are brown. Sprinkle with additional chopped parsley.

## Shrimp Scampi

**2 pounds raw shrimp**

**¾ cup olive oil**

**¾ teaspoon salt**

**½ teaspoon freshly ground black pepper**

**2 cloves garlic, minced**

**3 tablespoons minced parsley**

Wash shrimp shells and devein shrimp. Drain well. Mix oil, salt, pepper, garlic and parsley. Marinate shrimp for one hour, basting and turning frequently. Remove shrimp and thread on four or six skewers. Arrange on a baking sheet. Broil ten minutes.

## Olga's Spicy Shrimp

This recipe comes from Nana Mallett's recipe file. I don't know who Olga is.

**1 pound small cleaned shrimp**

**2 cloves garlic, crushed**

**2 tablespoons minced ginger**

**2 scallions, sliced**

**1 teaspoon chili paste**

**1 tablespoon soy sauce**

**1 teaspoon sugar**

**1 tablespoon wine**

**1 ½ tablespoons ketchup**

**2 tablespoon vegetable oil**

Deep fry shrimp for a minute and a half and drain. Stir ginger, garlic and scallions in heated vegetable oil one minute. Add shrimp to mixture. Stir and serve.

# Desserts

## Apple Crisp

**4 cups sliced pared apples**

**½ cup flour**

**½ cup sugar**

**½ cup butter**

**¼ cup water**

Preheat oven to 400 degrees.

Put apples in a buttered baking dish. Pour hot water over them. In a bowl, cream the sugar and flour into the butter to form crumbs. Sprinkle crumbs over apples and bake for 35 to 45 minutes.

## Blueberry Cobbler

**1 pint blueberries**

**⅓ cup sugar and ½ cup sugar**

**1 teaspoon grated lemon rind**

**⅔ cup water**

**¼ cup butter**

**1 cup flour**

**1 ½ teaspoon baking powder**

**¼ teaspoon salt**

**1 egg slightly beaten**

**½ cup milk**

**1 ½ teaspoon vanilla extract**

**Whipped cream/ice cream**

Combine berries, ⅓ sugar, rind and water in saucepan. Bring to boil. Stir to dissolve sugar. Simmer three minutes. Pour into a 1 ½ quart baking dish.

Cream butter. Gradually add ½ cup sugar. Beat until fluffy. Mix flour, baking powder and salt. Combine egg, milk and vanilla. Add dry ingredients to butter mixture, alternating with egg mixture, beating well after each addition. Spoon on top of hot berries. Bake 30 minutes. Serve with whipped cream or ice cream.

## Chocolate Mousse

**½ pound dark sweet chocolate cut into small pieces)**

**6 tablespoons coffee or water**

**5 eggs, separated**

**2 tablespoons rum**

Stir chocolate and coffee or water over low heat until chocolate melts. Beat egg yolks until thick and lemon colored. Slowly stir into chocolate. Stir in rum. Beat egg whites until stiff. Fold into chocolate mixture. Pour into eight small serving dishes. Chill at least four hours.

# Crepes I

⅔ cup sifted flour

1 tablespoon sugar

½ teaspoon salt

3 whole eggs

3 egg yolks

1 ½ cups milk

2 tablespoons butter or margarine, melted

1 tablespoon brandy

Sift together the flour, sugar, salt. Beat whole eggs and egg yolks well. Add milk, flour mixture, butter and brandy. Beat until smooth. Cover and refrigerate two hours. To cook crepes, add about ¼ cup butter to an oiled small (8 inch) skillet. Tip and tilt pan so that the batter will flow in a thin film over bottom. Cook. When lightly browned, turn and brown other side Place crepes between wax paper until ready to fill.

# Crepes II

1 ½ cups milk

2 eggs

1 cup flour

1 tablespoon oil

¼ teaspoon salt

**Butter or margarine**

In a blender, combine milk, eggs, flour, oil and salt. Cover and blend. Let stand 30 minutes. Heat a six-inch skillet over medium heat. Grease lightly with butter. Pour in ¼ cup batter; swirl to coat evenly. Pour off excess batter. Cook crepe until lightly brown. Flip and cook other side. Repeat until all batter is used. Stack crepes with wax paper between each crepe. Freeze any extra crepes. Yields 18 crepes.

## Indian Pudding

**4 cups milk**

**½ cup cornmeal**

**¾ teaspoon salt**

**1 teaspoon ginger**

**⅓ cup molasses**

Preheat oven to 325 degrees
Cook cornmeal and milk in a double boiler for 20 minutes. Add molasses, salt and ginger. Pour into buttered pudding dish and bake for two hours. Serve warm with ice cream.

## Aunt Mimi's Apricot Rice Pudding

**½ cup rice**

**½ cup sugar**

**½ teaspoon salt**

**3 cups milk**

**Grated rind of a half orange**

**2 eggs yolks**

**2 egg whites**

**1 cup canned or cooked apricots or fruit salad**

**4 tablespoons sugar**

Preheat oven to 300 degrees.

Cook rice in double boiler with milk until soft. Add sugar, yolks, salt and rind. Stir gently and cook until thick, about five minutes. Turn into buttered dish or pan. Cover top with fruit. Make meringue by beating whites and sugar. Spread over pudding. Bake about 15 minutes, long enough to brown meringue.

# 'Forever Summer' Offers Easy Cooking and Eating

Nigella Lawson seemed to be everywhere Following a whirlwind bicoastal media blitz, the former Deputy Literary Editor of England's " Sunday Times," who had written the popular weekly "At My Table" feature for "The New York Times'" Dining Out section, stopped by Borders in Fairfield, Connecticut in 2003 to promote her cookbook, "Forever Summer."

Dressed smartly in a long black skirt with black boots and a white sweater, it was easy to see why this international food writer has been called a "voluptuous upper-class foodie/beauty." The word *sensual* apply applies to her looks and to her recipes if one can believe her food critics.

Nearly 200 fans, from a mother holding infant twins, to a senior citizen gentleman from Scotland, lined up to meet and greet the journalist-turned-cookbook-author whose popularity has gained momentum for her down-to-earth approach to cooking.

Lawson, who was in the midst of her first American book tour, spent a few minutes talking with the media, before heading to Borders' second floor to meet her fans. "Despite what you see on television, cooking is not the province of the experts. Home cooking is real cooking. Just get into your kitchen. Try to demystify it," Lawson said

""Forever Summer" is typical of her cooking philosophy — "easy cooking and easy eating." The book has been described as "fresh, innovative, and versatile," offering summery recipes that can be eaten at any time — from succulent Spanish and Italian dishes to the fragrant mezze of the eastern Mediterranean; from roasted vegetables and barbecue sea bass to ice creams and cheesecake.

Lawson explained that it is the irony of television that has contributed to cooking becoming so unapproachable. A visual medium, television has put emphasis on the process and presentation, often overwhelming the average home cook.

The cookbook author believes cooking should be fun and a release in people's lives. She refers to her own professional life as an example and even the reason for her developing an interest and subsequent career in the food industry. While a working journalist, she would often find herself in the kitchen offering a respite and spawning ground for her as a writer. She found mixing ingredients freed up her mind and thought processes, resulting in her ability to write that first and all-too-important "first sentence."

During her newspaper career, she started writing restaurant reviews, but found it a daunting task. After her children were born, she started to spend more time at home and thought writing about cooking, rather than reviewing, would be less tasking. Her interest in food and cooking expanded into cookbook writing. Her books include "How to Eat: the Pleasures and Principles of Good Food;" "How to Be a Domestic Goddess," "Baking and the Art of Comfort Cooking;" "Nigella Bites," and "Forever Summer." Her books have sold in excess of two million copies worldwide.

In 1992, Lawson married the journalist and broadcaster John Diamond, who died from throat cancer in 2001. She lives in London with her two children.

When asked, which is one of her favorite recipes in "Forever Summer" Lawson said "Garlic and Lemon Chicken."

In the book, Lawson writes: "This is one of those recipes you just can't make once; that's to say, after the first time, you're hooked. It is gloriously easy; you just put everything in the roasting dish and leave it to cook in the oven, pervading the house, at any time of year, with the summer scent of lemon and thyme — and of course, and mellow, almost honeyed garlic."

Lawson's popularity stems from the fact that home cooks identify with her recipes. They're familiar and most of the recipes are easy and quick.

# Cakes, Cookies and Pies

## Apple Cake

**3 eggs**

**1¾ cup sugar**

**7 ounces vegetable oil**

**1 teaspoon vanilla**

**2 cups flour**

**1 teaspoon baking soda**

**1 teaspoon cinnamon**

**1 teaspoon salt**

**3 cups sliced McIntosh apples**

**Additional sugar for topping**

Preheat oven to 350 degree

Beat eggs with sugar.  Add oil and vanilla. Mix flour, baking soda, cinnamon and salt, and then add to egg mixture.  Add apples. Pour into a 9"x13" pan. Bake for 45 to 50 minutes. Sprinkle with sugar while warm.


## Banana Bread

**½ cup nuts**

**1 cup mashed banana (2)**

**1 ½ sifted all-purpose flour**

**1 teaspoon baking soda**

½ teaspoon salt

½ cup soft butter

1 cup sugar

2 eggs

1 teaspoon vanilla or ½ teaspoon lemon extract

½ cup sour cream or ¼ cup buttermilk

Preheat oven to 350 degrees.

Chop nuts. Mash bananas. Sift together flour, baking soda and salt. Combine butter, sugar, egg and flavoring. Cream for 1 ½ minutes. Add banana, sour cream, nuts and flour mixture. Beat until blended. Grease a 9"x5"x3" pan. Fill with batter. Bake for one hour.


**Carrot Cake**

4 eggs

2 cups sugar

3 small baby food jars of strained carrots (4 oz.)

1 cup vegetable oil

1 teaspoon vanilla

2 cups all-purpose flour

2 teaspoons baking soda

2 teaspoons cinnamon

1 teaspoon salt

1 small can crushed pineapple, drained

1 cup chopped walnuts

1 cup white or golden raisins


Frosting – if you wish, or just sprinkle powdered sugar on top of cake

3 ounce package cream cheese

1/3 stick of butter or margarine

3 tablespoons evaporated milk or light cream

Confectioner's sugar, for desired spreading consistency


Preheat oven 400 degrees

Combine eggs and sugar, and beat until light. Add strained carrots, oil and vanilla. Sift together the flour, baking soda, cinnamon, and salt.  Add to batter and beat until thoroughly mixed. Add pineapple, walnuts and raisins. Bake in a tube pan for ten minutes. Reduce heat to 350 degrees and continue baking for 55 minutes. Cool. Top with frosting.


**Cheese Cake I**


1 pound cream cheese

1 ¼ pounds butter

1 ½ cups sugar

1 pound ricotta

4 eggs

4 tablespoons cornstarch

**4 tablespoons flour**

**1 tablespoon vanilla**

**1 pint sour cream**

Preheat oven 325 degrees

Beat together until smooth, the cream cheese, butter and sugar. Add ricotta, eggs, flour, cornstarch and vanilla. Beat until smooth. Add sour cream and beat again. Butter a 9-inch spring pan. Sprinkle with graham cracker crumbs and pour in filling. Bake for 1 hour and 15 minutes. Open oven door and leave cake in to cool.

**Cheese Cake II**

## Crust

**1 ½ cups graham cracker crumbs**

**¼ cup sugar**

**6 to 8 tablespoons melted butter**

**1 teaspoon cinnamon**

Mix above ingredients. Press ¾ of the mixture on bottom and partially up sides of a 10-inch springboard pan.

## Filling

**2 pounds cream cheese (softened for 6 to 8 hours)**

**4 eggs, well beaten**

**1 cup sugar**

**½ pint sour cream**

**⅛ teaspoon salt**

**1 tablespoon lemon juice**

Preheat oven 325 to 350 degrees.

Beat eggs and sugar until thick and lemon-colored. Set aside. Cream the cheese. Add sour cream to cream cheese. Blend well. Add eggs and sugar mixture to the cream cheese mixture. Beat well. Pour into pan. Bake for approximately one hour and 15 minutes. Test with toothpick. If too moist, continue baking until done.

## Topping (optional)

**½ pint sour cream**

**2 tablespoons sugar**

**½ to 1 teaspoon vanilla**

Mix and spread over nearly baked cake. Sprinkle with remaining graham cracker crumbs and bake in hot oven for ten minutes. Cool and place in refrigerator overnight. Remove one hour before serving.

## Aunt Jennie's Cheese Cake

**1 ½ cup graham cracker crumbs**

**¼ cup sugar**

**¼ cup melted butter**

**1 pound cream cheese**

1 teaspoon vanilla

½ cup sugar

3 eggs

**Mixture:**

1 pint sour cream

¼ cup sugar

1 teaspoon vanilla

Preheat oven to 375 degrees.

Mix graham crackers crumbs, sugar and butter, and put in a greased pie dish. Chill 15 minutes. Mix cream cheese, vanilla, sugar and eggs. Pour into shell. Bake 20 minutes. Cool 20 minutes. Increase oven temperature to 450 degrees. Mix sour cream, sugar and vanilla and spread onto cake. Bake 10 minutes.

**Mary's Cheese Cake**

**<u>Basic Crumb Crust</u>**

**2 pounds cream cheese**

**¾ cup sugar**

**2 eggs, lightly beaten**

**1 teaspoon vanilla**

**2 teaspoons cornstarch**

**1 cup sour cream**

**2 cans Bing cherries, drained**

**Currant jelly**

Preheat oven to 450 degrees

Beat together cream cheese and sugar until smooth and light. Beat in the eggs, vanilla and cornstarch only until thoroughly mixed. Stir in the sour cream until the mixture is well blended. Pour the mixture into the prepared crust and bake for 45 minutes. Allow the cake to cool in the oven with the door propped slightly open for 3 hours. Chill. Melt currant jelly and add cherries. Spread atop cake.

**Midget Cheese Cake**

**¼ cup butter**

**¾ cup graham crackers crumbs**

**1 tablespoon sugar**

**8 ounces cream cheese**

**1 egg**

**1 tablespoon vanilla**

**¼ cup sugar**

Preheat oven to 375 degrees

Mix together the butter, crumbs and sugar and place in midget cupcake papers ¼ inch deep. Beat together the cream cheese, egg, vanilla and sugar. Fill each cupcake liner to the top with the cream cheese mixture. Bake for 10 to 12 minutes. Top as desired. Chill.

## Italian Flourless Chocolate Cake

7 tablespoons unsalted butter softened, plus more for pan

½ cup confectioner's sugar, sifted, plus more for dusting

4 ounces, "top quality" dark chocolate

2 extra-large eggs, separated

2 tablespoons potato starch

3 ½ tablespoons superfine sugar

Preheat oven to 350 degrees.

Butter an 8-inch cake pan. Line bottom with parchment.

In a large bowl, using a mixer or by hand, beat the 7 tablespoons butter with the confectioner's sugar until smooth and creamy. Melt chocolate in a pan on top of stove. Pour warm chocolate over the butter and sugar mixture and beat until smooth. Whisk in egg yolks one at a time. Stir in potato starch.

In a medium bowl, beat egg whites until soft peaks form. Gradually beat in superfine sugar and continue beating until firm peaks develop. Fold egg whites into chocolate mixture.

Scrape the batter out of the bowl, and spread it in the pan. Bake for 18 minutes. Cake will rise and top will look dry and a little crackly. Remove pan from oven. Place on a rack and allow to cool completely, about 2 hours. Cake will sink a bit.

Unmold cake; peel off parchment; then invert onto a serving dish so the crackly surface is on top. Generously sift Confectioner's sugar over the top; then serve.

(This recipe is adapted from a recipe from Cusina E. Butega Restaurant in Ferrara, Italy. I first tasted a flourless cake a few years ago following a meeting of the book club that I had belonged to at the time in Massachusetts. I was so fascinated by the creamy chocolate inside of this cake. I made the cake after I saw this recipe in a newspaper.)

## Coffee Cake

**1 ½ cups – less 2 tablespoons flour**

**2 teaspoons baking powder**

**½ teaspoon salt**

**½ cup sugar**

**1 egg, beaten**

**½ cup milk**

**3 tablespoons melted butter**

Preheat oven to 400 degrees

Sift together the flour, baking powder, salt and sugar. Combine with egg, milk and butter. Beat until smooth. Pour into 8" by 8" buttered pan. Dot with butter rolled in sugar. Sprinkle with sugar. Bake for 25 minutes.

## Angie's Mini Cranberry Cupcakes

**½ cup butter or margarine**

**1 ½ cups firmly packed brown sugar**

**1 egg**

**1 ½ cups (12 ounces) cottage cheese**

**1 cup raisins**

2 cups fresh or frozen fresh cranberries, rinsed and drained (cut the cranberries in 2 to 3 pieces).

2 ½ cups unsifted all–purpose flour

1 teaspoon salt

½ teaspoon baking soda

1 cup finely cut walnuts, optional

Confectioner's sugar

Preheat oven to 350 degrees.

In a bowl, cream butter until light and fluffy. Stir in sugar, egg and cottage cheese. Fold in raisins and cranberries.  Add walnuts. Stir in flour, salt and baking soda. Spoon batter into 24 mini cupcake liners in muffin pan. (Regular cupcakes, fill ¾; mini cups fill to the top.) Bake 30 to 35 minutes or until puffed and brown. Sprinkle confectioner's sugar on top of muffin.


## Cream Cheese Cupcakes

3 8-ounce packages of cream cheese

5 eggs

1 cup sugar

1 teaspoon vanilla


### Filling

1 pint sour cream

4 tablespoons sugar

1 teaspoon vanilla

**Cherries for garnish**

Preheat oven to 300 degrees

Soften cream cheese. Add eggs one at a time alternating with sugar and vanilla. Line cupcake tins with paper cups. Fill ⅔ full. Bake for 40 minutes. Remove from oven. Wait a few minutes until cupcakes sink a little. Top each with about a tablespoon of filling and then with a cherry. Put back in the oven for another five minutes. Remove from oven; cool. Refrigerate.


**Cream Puffs**

**1 cup boiling water**

**½ cup shortening, butter or margarine**

**½ teaspoon salt**

**1 cup sifted flour**

**4 eggs beaten**

**Whipped cream or cream pie filling**

**Confectioner's sugar**

Preheat oven to 450 F

Add shortening and salt to boiling water and heat to boiling. Reduce heat. Add flour all at once and stir vigorously until mixture forms a ball around spoon and then leaves spoon clean. Remove from heat. Add one egg at a time to mixture, beating very thoroughly after each addition. Continue beating until mixture is thick and shiny, and breaks from spoon.

Depending upon desired size, spoon 1 teaspoon or 1 tablespoon of mixture onto an ungreased cookie sheet.

Bake in a very hot oven for 10 minutes. Reduce heat to moderate (350 F) and bake about 20 minutes longer. Cool. Make slit on one side of each puff and fill with whipped cream or cream pie filling. Sprinkle each puff with sifted confectioner's sugar.

Makes 1 dozen large or 4 dozen small puffs.

**Orange Rum Cake**

This is one of my favorite holiday cakes, especially for Thanksgiving. The best part is that the cake can be made days before the holiday and kept in the pan until it is time for serving.

**1 cup butter or margarine (salted, not whipped)**

**2 cups sugar**

**Grated rind of 2 large oranges and 1 lemon**

**2 eggs**

**2 ½ cups sifted all-purpose flour**

**2 teaspoons double acting baking powder**

**1 teaspoon baking soda**

**½ teaspoon salt**

**1 cup buttermilk**

**1 cup finely chopped walnuts or pecans**

**Juice of 2 large oranges**

**Juice of 1 lemon**

**2 tablespoons rum**

**Walnut or pecan halves. Optional**

Preheat oven to 350 degrees

Mix together flour, baking powder, baking soda and salt. Set aside. Cream butter, 1 cup sugar and orange and lemon peel until fluffy. Add eggs, one at a time, and beat after each until blended. Add flour mixture alternately with buttermilk. Fold in walnuts. Grease 9-inch tube pan. Spread batter into pan. Bake approximately one hour. Cool pan on rack slightly. In saucepan, mix juices, remaining 1 cup sugar and rum. Bring to a boil. Pour over cake in pan. Add walnut or pecan slice on top of cake. Cool and cover. Let cake stand in pan a day or two before serving.

## Old-Fashioned Pound Cake

**1 pound (4 cups) confectioner's sugar**

**2 cups (1 pound) margarine**

**2 tablespoons grated orange rind**

**6 eggs**

**3 ½ cups flour**

**¼ teaspoon salt**

Preheat oven to 350 degrees

Sift sugar. Cream margarine. Add sugar and rind to margarine and cream thoroughly. Add eggs, one at a time, mixing well after each addition. Gradually add combined flour and salt. Mix well. Pour into greased and floured 10-inch tube pan. Bake for one hour and 20 minutes. Remove from pan.

## Sour Cream Pound Cake

1 cup butter

2 ¾ cups sugar

6 eggs

3 cups sifted flour

½ teaspoon salt

¼ teaspoon baking soda

1 cup sour cream

1 teaspoon vanilla

Preheat oven to 350 degrees

Cream butter and sugar until light. Add eggs one at a time. Add vanilla to sour cream. Alternating with dry ingredients add sour cream to butter and sugar. Pour batter into a greased 9-inch tube pan lined with wax paper. Bake for 1 hour and 10 minutes.


## Struffoli (Italian Honey Balls)

1 ½ cups sifted all-purpose flour

6 eggs

1 teaspoon salt

1 3 ounce bottle confetti sprinkles

1 one pound bottle honey

6 tablespoons sugar

**Fat for frying**

Mix flour, eggs and salt together in a bowl until the dough cleans the bowl. (Add another cup of flour if necessary). Knead on a lightly floured board until dough is smooth and does not stick to the fingers. Cut small pieces from dough; roll into long narrow ropes and cut into 1/8 or ¼ inch pieces. Roll each piece between palms into tiny balls. Fry a handful at a time in deep, hot fat (use a clean solid or liquid vegetable shortening) until golden brown.

Drain on paper towels. Meanwhile in large saucepan, heat honey and sugar until mixture is warm. Place the drained honey balls in this saucepan and mix until all are coated with honey. Remove. Form balls into a ring on a dish. Top with candy confetti sprinkles and/or orange peel, nuts and slivered almonds. Let cool and serve.

Note: This is a very traditional sweet dessert from my Italian-American heritage. It is a festive-looking complement to the holiday dessert table, especially at Christmas time.

## Sugar and Spice Christmas Cake

I found this recipe on a typed piece of paper in my recipe file. Someone had sent me the recipe with the salutation, "Dear Rita, I hope you enjoy this recipe." I don't know who sent it to me. The person noted that "this is our tried and true sour cream pound cake that has the batter layered in the tube pan with sugar and spice and chopped walnuts, but with a difference – the beer. If anything, it is lighter and finer textured. It's a nice cake to have ready during the holidays for drop-in guests."

I wonder, do people really drop in anymore?

**¾ cup butter or margarine**

**1 ½ teaspoons vanilla**

1 ½ cups sugar

3 eggs

1 ½ cups sour cream

3 cups unsifted flour

1 ½ teaspoons baking powder

1 ½ teaspoons baking soda

½ teaspoon salt

½ cup beer

⅔ cup chopped walnuts

½ cup sugar

2 teaspoons cinnamon


Preheat oven to 350 degrees

In a bowl, cream butter or margarine until light. Gradually beat in sugar. Beat in eggs, one at a time. Add vanilla and sour cream. Combine flour with baking powder, baking soda and salt, and add to creamed mixture, alternately with the beer. Mix until silky smooth batter is achieved. In a small bowl, mix chopped walnuts with sugar and cinnamon.

Spoon one-third of cake batter into a well-greased tube pan (10 in.). Scatter ⅓ of the walnut mixture over batter in the pan. Repeat layering with batter and nut mixture twice. Bake in oven for one hour or until cake tester inserted in cake comes away clean. Let cake cool in pan on rack.

## Wasps

**1 ½ cups sugar**

**½ cup water**

**6 egg whites**

**1 pound powdered sugar**

**1 pound pecans**

**Vanilla extract**

Preheat oven to 350 degrees

Boil sugar and water until light brown about 5 to 8 minutes. Cool slightly. Beat egg whites until stiff. Add powdered sugar gradually to egg whites. Beat until light. Add sugar and white mixture. Beat well. Add one pound pecans and a few drops vanilla. Drop by teaspoon onto greased sheet. Bake for 12 to 15 minutes.

## Applesauce Cookies

**1 cup shortening**

**2 cups sugar**

**1 egg**

**3 cups flour**

**1 teaspoon cinnamon**

**½ teaspoon cloves**

**1 teaspoon salt**

**1 teaspoon baking soda**

**1 cup unsweetened applesauce**

**1 cup nuts**

**½ cup seedless raisins**

**1 teaspoon vanilla**

Preheat oven to 375 degrees.

Cream the shortening. Add sugar gradually and cream until fluffy. Add egg and beat. Sift flour and then sift again with dry ingredients. Fold into batter. Add applesauce, nuts, raisins, and vanilla. Mix. Drop by teaspoon onto greased cookie sheet. Bake for 15 to 20 minutes.

## Bows

**2 ¼ cups flour**

**2 eggs**

**2 egg yolks**

**1 tablespoon rum**

**⅛ teaspoon salt**

**Confectioner's sugar**

**Vegetable oil**

Place two cups flour in bowl. Make a well. Add eggs, egg yolks, rum, confectioner's sugar and salt. Mix. Form dough into a rough ball. Sprinkle rest of flour on board. Knead. Refrigerate for one hour. Heat 2 to 4 inches of oil in pan. Roll out one-quarter dough at a time. Cut into thick strips, 7 inches long and ½ inch wide. Tie into loose knots. Deep fry one to two minutes. Drain. Sprinkle with sugar before serving.

## Forgotten Cookies

**2 egg whites**

**⅔ cup sugar**

**1 cup chocolate bits**

**1 cup chopped walnuts**

**1 teaspoon vanilla**

**Pinch of salt**

Preheat oven to 350 degrees.

Beat egg whites until foamy. Add sugar and beat until stiff. Add chocolate, walnuts, vanilla and salt. Mix together. Line cookie sheet with foil and lightly grease foil. Spoon onto cookie sheet. Place in oven. Turn off oven immediately. Leave in oven overnight.

Variation: You may use mint-flavored chocolate bits and green coloring for the holidays.

## Lemon Bars

**2 cups sifted all-purpose flour**

**½ cup sifted confectioner's sugar**

**1 cup butter**

**¼ cup all-purpose flour**

**4 eggs beaten**

**2 cups sugar**

**⅓ cup lemon juice**

½ teaspoon baking powder

Preheat oven to 350 degrees

Sift together 2 cups flour and ½ cup confectioner's sugar. Cut in butter until mixture clings together. Press into a 13 x 9 two-inch pan. Bake for 15-20 minutes until lightly browned. Beat together eggs, sugar and lemon juice. Sift together the ¼ cup- flour and baking powder. Stir into egg mixture. Pour over baked crust. Bake for 25 minutes longer. Sprinkle with confectioner's sugar and cool. Cut into bars.

## Peanut Butter Cookies

¾ cup unsalted butter, softened

1 ½ cups peanut butter

½ cup sugar

¾ cup firmly packed brown sugar

1 egg

1 teaspoon vanilla extract

1 ½ cups flour

1 teaspoon baking soda

¼ teaspoon salt

Preheat oven to 375 degrees.

Lightly grease cookie sheets. Beat the butter and peanut butter together in bowl until creamy. Add the sugars gradually, beating until light. Beat in the egg and vanilla. Mix the flour, baking soda and salt and stir into the butter mixture making a smooth dough.

Shape the dough into balls the size of a walnut, and place them on cookie sheets about 1/2 inch apart. Press the dough balls flat with a fork. Bake the cooks until firm and lightly brown about 10 to 12 minutes.

## Peanut Butter Drop Cookies

**1 cup peanut butter**

**1 cup sugar**

**1 egg**

**1 teaspoon vanilla**

Preheat oven to 325 degrees

Combine all ingredients; drop by tablespoon onto a greased cookie sheet. Bake for 10 minutes. Makes 40 cookies.

## Unbaked Peanut Butter Cookies

**½ cup white sugar**

**½ cup white syrup (Karo)**

**1 cup peanut butter**

**3 ½ cups cornflakes**

Bring sugar and syrup to a boil only to dissolve sugar. Stir and do not overcook. Remove from heat and add peanut butter. Stir well. Add cornflakes. Stir well. Drop by small amounts from teaspoon onto wax paper. Makes about 40 cookies.

## Helen Farwell's Peanut Butter Cookies

1 cup white sugar

1 cup brown sugar

1 cup shortening

2 eggs

A pinch of salt

1 cup peanut butter

3 cups sifted flour

Preheat oven to 375 degrees

Mix all ingredients and roll pieces of dough into a ball, the size of walnuts; form into a cookie shape. Bake on an ungreased cookie sheet for ten minutes. Makes six dozen.

## Snowballs

2 ¼ cups sifted flour

½ pound butter

½ cup confectioner's sugar

1 cup finely chopped nuts

1 teaspoon vanilla

Preheat oven to 350 degrees

Combine all ingredients and form into balls the size of a walnut. Bake for 20 minutes. Roll in confectioner's sugar. Makes three dozen.

## Cousin Rose's Sour Cream Cookies

**1 pound butter**

**1 cup sugar**

**2 eggs**

**5 cups flour**

**½ teaspoon salt**

**1 teaspoon baking soda**

**16 ounce sour cream**

**Icing:**

**1 box confectioner's sugar**

**1 teaspoon vanilla**

Preheat oven to 375 degrees

Mix butter, sugar and eggs.  Mix flour, salt, baking soda and sour cream. Add to butter mixture. Drop by tablespoon onto a greased cookie sheet. Bake for 15 to 20 minutes or until lightly brown. Mix confectioner's sugar and vanilla with a little water to spread easily on cooled cookies.

## Stay-Up-All-Night Cookies

**2 egg whites**

**⅔ cup sugar**

**½ teaspoon vanilla**

**Speck of salt**

**1 cup chocolate bits**

Beat egg whites until stiff. Slowly add sugar, vanilla and salt to the egg whites. Stir in the chocolate bits. Heat oven to 375 degrees and then turn off. Drop batter by small amounts onto cookie sheet. Place in oven all night or at least six hours. Makes 48 cookies.

**Sugar Cookies**

**1 cup butter**

**1 cup sugar**

**3 eggs**

**3 ½ cups sifted flour**

**2 teaspoons baking powder**

**1 ½ teaspoons vanilla**

Preheat oven to 350 degrees

Cream butter. Gradually add sugar and continue creaming. Add eggs and beat well. Blend in sifted dry ingredients and vanilla extract. Bake until cookies are done.

**Bran Muffins**

**1 cup flour**

**3 ½ teaspoons baking powder**

½ teaspoon salt

2 tablespoons brown sugar

1 cup bran

1 egg beaten

⅔ cup milk

2 tablespoons melted shortening

Raisins, optional


Preheat 425 degrees.

Mix flour, baking powder and salt. Stir in the sugar and bran. Combine the beaten egg, milk and shortening. Add to the dry ingredients and mix quickly. Bake for 25 minutes.


## Raisin Bran Muffins

1 ¼ cups flour

3 teaspoons baking powder

½ teaspoon salt

½ cup sugar

3 cups raisin bran

1 ¼ cups milk

1 egg

⅓ cup vegetable oil


Preheat oven to 400 degrees

Stir together the flour, baking powder, salt and sugar. Set aside. Mix raisin bran and milk in a bowl. Let stand one to two minutes or until cereal is softened. Add egg and vegetable oil. Beat well. Add dry ingredients to cereal mixture stirring only until combined. Portion batter evenly into 12 greased 2 ½ inch muffin pan cups. Bake for 25 minutes or until muffins are golden brown. Serve warm. Yields 12 muffins.

## Pie Crust (100 Years)

**2 ½ cups flour**

**1 teaspoon salt**

**¼ cup sugar**

**1 cup shortening**

**½ cup milk**

Sift flour, salt and sugar. Cut in shortening. Add milk and mix lightly, but thoroughly. Roll out.

## Swedish Apple Pie

**Sliced peeled apples (enough to fill pie plate three-quarters)**

**1 tablespoon sugar**

**1 tablespoon cinnamon**

**¾ tablespoon melted butter**

**1 cup sugar**

**1 egg, beaten**

**¼ cup chopped nuts**

**Pinch of salt**

Preheat oven to 350 degrees

Fill pie plate with apples. Sprinkle with sugar and cinnamon. In a small bowl, combine butter, sugar, egg, nuts and salt. Pour over apples. Bake for 45 minutes or until golden brown.

**Shaker Lemon Pie**

**2 large lemons**

**4 eggs, well beaten**

**2 cups sugar**

**2 pie crusts for a 9-inch pie**

Preheat oven to 450 degrees

Slice lemons paper thin. Combine the lemons with sugar and mix well. Let stand two hours or overnight. Blend occasionally. Add the beaten egg to lemon mixture and mix well. Turn into pie plate, arranging slices evenly. Cover with top crust and cut several slits near center. Bake for 15 minutes. Reduce heat to 375 degrees and bake 20 minutes or until a knife inserted into pie comes out clean.

**Nana's Mincemeat Pie**

**2 cups prepared mincemeat or one 9-ounce package**

**2 cups thinly sliced pared tart apples**

**¼ teaspoon grated lemon peel**

## Pastry for two 8-inch pie crust

Preheat oven to 450 degrees

If using prepared mincemeat, prepare according to package directions. Combine mincemeat, apples and grated lemon peel. Line pie plates with pastry. Pour in filling. Adjust top crust and crimp edges. With knife cut design in crust. Sprinkle lightly with sugar. Bake for 35 minutes. Serve warm.

## Frozen Peanut Butter Pie

**3 ounces cream cheese**

**1 cup confectioner's sugar**

**⅓ cup creamy peanut butter**

**½ cup milk**

**1 cup Cool Whip**

**1 9" pie crust**

Whip cheese until soft and fluffy. Beat in sugar and peanut butter. Slowly add milk, blending thoroughly. Fold in Cool Whip. Pour mixture into a baked pie shell. Sprinkle with ¼ cup chopped nuts. Freeze and serve.

## Nana's Peanut Butter Chiffon Pie

**1 envelope unflavored gelatin**

**½ cup sugar**

**¼ teaspoon salt**

1 cup milk

2 eggs, separated

⅔ cup smooth peanut butter

1 cup sour cream

9-inch pie shell, baked

In top part of small double boiler, mix gelatin, ¼ cup sugar and salt. Add milk and egg yolks, and beat until blended. Put over simmering water and cook, stirring until mixture thickens slightly and coats spoon. Remove from heat and pour into bowl. Beat in peanut butter. Cool thoroughly. Beat egg whites until foamy. Gradually add remaining sugar and beat until stiff Stir sour cream into peanut butter mixture. Then, fold in egg whites. Pile lightly into pie shell and chill until firm.


## Nana's Pumpkin Pie

1 ½ cups canned or mashed cooked pumpkin

¾ cup sugar

½ teaspoon salt

1 teaspoon cinnamon

½ to 1 teaspoon ginger

¼ to ½ teaspoon nutmeg

¼ to ½ teaspoon cloves

3 slightly beaten eggs

1 ¼ cups milk

1 6-ounce can evaporated milk

**9" unbaked pastry shell.**

Preheat oven to 400 degrees

Combine pumpkin, sugar, salt and spices. Blend in eggs, milk and evaporated milk. Pour mixture into an unbaked pastry shell. Have edges crimped high. Bake for 50 minutes or until knife inserted halfway between center and outside comes out clean.

**Etc.**

# Greenwoods' Muesli

This recipe comes from Deanna Raymond, a former Fairfield, Connecticut, resident who formerly owned a Bed and Breakfast Inn in Norfolk, Connecticut. I had written a feature about Deanna and her B & B and stayed at the inn in the 1980s. She served this Muesli at breakfast and graciously gave me her recipe.

**2 cups rolled oats (uncooked)**

**1 cup orange juice**

**1 cup milk**

**1 cup yogurt**

**Raisins**

**Chopped almonds**

**1 apple chopped**

Stir the above ingredients together. Serve with additional fruit on the side.

# Holidays

# Setting a Place at Holiday Table for Those No Longer With Us

It's a bittersweet time of year, isn't it? We are busy preparing for the holidays, with last-minute shopping for gifts and food for the holiday meal. We are happy anticipating the joy of getting together with friends and family. Yet, as with any holiday or special occasion, we usually take a moment to think back to other celebrations with family members and become nostalgic or even sad as the memories stop us in our tracks. We may be shopping in a store when that special holiday song will come over the loudspeaker. Or, we may be in the kitchen, the day before Christmas, prepping the dinner for the family get-together.

Of course, it is not just the holidays that bring to mind the family members no longer with us, and it is not just the memories that creep in and stir something in our brain often times so unexpectedly. It is the little things that maybe we intentionally keep around us, so that our family remains close to us in some way. We feel them. They comfort us, as I say, in the little ways.

I wonder how many objects people keep in their homes that once belonged to family members. They've become so much part of their lives today that they don't realize the subconscious comfort as they go about their day.

This brings to mind the country music song, "I Drive Your Truck," which won a country music award a few years ago. The lyrics are based on a true story of the father of Sgt. 1st Class Jared Monti of Massachusetts, who was killed in action in Afghanistan in 2006. He was awarded the Medal of Honor, and his father now drives his 2001 Dodge Ram 1500. During an interview, the father said that it was his way of holding on to something of his son's.

My friend Sara Sikes recalls that years ago, when her mother died, she had convinced her father to sell her mother's car to her. "He had a hard time letting go of it, even though we live in the same town," but he did, she said. "I used to feel very close to her when I drove it."

We all have our ways.

Yes, we all have our ways, especially during the holidays when we look around our homes and our family table, only to be surprised how, in little ways, we bring deceased family members to the dinner table.

# Thanksgiving Dinner Continues Family Traditions

I can still see the wine glasses—three-quarters full with mulled cider and a cinnamon stick resting inside the glass—set in the middle of the dinner plate. My, how proud I felt to host my first Thanksgiving dinner in my new home, a three bedroom ranch-styled house in Greenlawn, Long Island. It was 1965 and my first born, a daughter was just two months old.

I spent a month preparing and planning the dinner which I would host just for my parents. I remember first baking an orange-rum cake, weeks before the special holiday. The recipe called for drizzling rum on the cake every few days and letting it just sit ahead of time. I've saved that recipe for years, a reminder of my first Thanksgiving as a young mother and how proud I was to welcome my parents to my first home where we would live for only three years until my husband's job, as an employee of Dun and Bradstreet, offered him a promotion, a new position as a regional sales manager in St. Louis, Missouri.

I served our first Thanksgiving on a wrought iron dining room set that I still have. It was painted aqua and complemented with sheer aqua curtains on the bowed dining room window that looked out to a typical Long Island plot of grass, just large enough for children to play. The yard backed up to a gladiola farm; who could ask for a more beautiful backdrop to our first home.

I had planned the dinner menu patterned after the one my mother would serve years past: turkey, stuffing, creamed onions, mashed potatoes, sweet potatoes whipped and topped with marshmallows, and cranberry sauces. Years later, I would make my own cranberry sauce with ground cranberries and pieces of orange—a project I would do with my three children as we took out my mother's old food grinder — the kind you clamp onto the side of a table or counter to affix before grinding – tedious, but fun with children. And yes, a little messy.

The joy of planning a Thanksgiving dinner is really in the process – the process of planning the menu, shopping for the ingredients and cooking. Then, of course, it is observing the family as everyone sits down before each place setting with the "good" dinner plates and silver flatware worthy of the meal.

The best part of my first Thanksgiving as a young mother, of course, was how proud I was to serve the holiday dinner to my parents, especially my father who would always walk around the house with a touch of pride that his daughter was now living in her own home and with her own family.

Thanksgiving continues to be my favorite holiday. I no longer host the dinner, for it is more comfortable to be in one of my children's homes. However, I enjoy participating in the planning and cooking, so that I can contribute the side dishes that have become part of the Thanksgiving tradition in my family. These traditions really began with the dinners I remember growing up.

As with other holiday dinners, the Thanksgiving meal continues family traditions and creates new ones to be passed along to future generations.

## My Family's Traditional Thanksgiving Menu

Turkey
Stuffing
Cranberry Sauce
Mashed Potatoes
Sweet Potatoes
Creamed White Onions
Green Beans

Desserts – Orange Rum Cake, Apple Pie, Pumpkin Pie

# Lidia's 'Nonna Tell Me a Story'

Even if you don't know Italian, you will probably recognize "Tutti a tavola a mangiare!"—the familiar signature closing to Lidia Bastianich's popular public television series in which she invites "Everyone to the table to eat."

Known by her fans as simply "Lidia," the 63-year-old television personality enjoys extending an invitation during the holiday season in the form of a children's book "Nonna Tell Me A Story: Lidia's Christmas Kitchen." In her book, she invites families to gather together to share their own memories of holiday traditions, as she shares her own memories with readers. Her first children's picture book includes 15 holiday recipes and tree-trimming advice.

The James Beard Award-winning chef, best-selling cookbook author, restaurateur and owner of a flourishing food and entertainment business, debuted her children's book in 2010 at a talk and book-signing at R. J. Julia Booksellers in Madison, Connecticut. Her local appearance attracted over 75 fans who took advantage of the opportunity to ask this grandmother of five some of the secrets of her Italian cooking success.

Dressed in black pants and sweater with a cascading long fringed red wool scarf accenting the festive holiday season, Lidia greeted her audience with her familiar conversational tone. It is this familiarity in her approach that has drawn fans to Lidia's television programs, her cookbooks, her restaurants and most recently to Eataly, an Italian-food market and restaurant complex that opened in 2010 at 200 Fifth Avenue between 23rd and 24th Street, with her son Joseph Bastianich, and Oscar Farinetti, who originally conceived the market and restaurant concept in Turin, Italy and brought it to New York in partnership with the Bastianich family.

"Nonna Tell Me A Story" is a story within a story. Lidia recounts to her own five grandchildren her childhood memories in Italy when she, her brother and parents visited Lidia's grandparents to celebrate Christmas. Lidia's grandchildren call her "Nonni," which she says is an "endearing" way of calling her "grandma" in Italian. Her own mother, Ermina, 90, lives with Lidia and is referred to as "Nonna Mima."

The book is beautifully illustrated by Laura Logan who captures Lidia, as a young child, visiting her grandparents' house, "set around a courtyard. And my, that courtyard was a whole world in itself." Lidia and her brother Franco "would scout out the best juniper bush for our Christmas tree." In her picture book, Lidia describes how as a little girl she would help her Nonna Rosa make little wreaths from dried figs and bay leaves. They would tie fresh fruit, including tangerines, small apples and Seckel pears to the tree. Growing up in Istria, the family didn't have much, but they would creatively make use of what the land provided. Christmas was more about being together than presents.

Lidia writes: "We didn't have fancy colored lights back then...We put tiny candies all over the tree. They came in shiny wrappers of different colors that shone like little gems among the branches."

In the storybook, when Lidia finishes recounting the Italian holiday celebration, she and her grandchildren set to work creating new memories with Nonna Lidia as they decorate the Christmas tree and bake cookies. A key illustration depicts Lidia with her daughter Tanya and her husband and two children, along with her son Joseph, his wife and three children and Nonna Mima sitting around the Christmas tree. Lidia's grandchildren include Julia, 7, Ethan, 8, Miles, 9, Lorenzo, 10 and Olivia, 12.

"This is a story that brings families and friends together," Lidia told her audience in Madison soon after commenting how "it was a nice ride up, a little trafficky." She noted to her audience that when she left her home, her 90-year old mother asked what time she would be home.

Lidia, whose cookbooks include "Lidia Cooks from the Heart of Italy and Lidia's Italy"—both companion books to the Emmy-nominated PBS series, wrote the children's book so that she could share some memories of the holiday season with her own grandchildren, whose facial features the artist Logan captured in the illustrations. "That way we involved the children as well," Lidia said.

"Oh, Grandma, I don't smile like that," one of her grandchildren told her after seeing how she was depicted, Lidia recalled.

"I hope the book is something that should be kept as a reference in the kitchen," said Lidia, who described some of the recipes,

204

such as "Angel Food Cupcakes" as "more contemporary." Also, she said she kept the focus on the nutritional aspects and therefore included some flourless recipes, "recipes that had been out there that I had modified."

In the introduction to her book, Lidia writes:

"Wherever your family comes from, whether privileged or less fortunate, I am sure there are special holiday traditions that you honor each year. I hope what I share in this book will encourage you and your family to celebrate, and bring simple heartfelt warmth into your own holidays. Perhaps you will discover a favorite recipe or two, and start a new tradition of baking or cooking them together each year."

In addition, Lidia offers one message "to every child of the world...May their food be healthy and grown in harmony with the earth and its seasons."

# Postscript

# Change at the Grand Union Meant More Than Coins

*In 1995, my local Grand Union in Fairfield, Connecticut, closed its doors after more than 50 years on the Post Road at the corner of South Benson Road. I had shopped at the supermarket for 25 years. At its closing, I wrote an essay about the change that led me to reflect upon the changes in my own food shopping and my life during the quarter of a century leading up to the closing. Here is that reflection.*

The supermarket is a place where change—both large and light—has been registered in my life.

For the past 25 years, Grand Union on the Post Road was where I bought the baby food, the peanut butter and jelly for school lunches and the chicken for weekend barbecues. Grand Union was where I pushed mountains of groceries down aisle after aisle between PTA meetings and writing assignments. Grand Union was where, over the years, I watched the mountain of breakfast cereals, cold cuts, cans of Betty Crocker cherry icing and boxes of jello and chocolate pudding dwindle to boxes of frozen pizzas, packaged hamburger patties and jars of prepared spaghetti sauce as my life and those of my family changed. Grand Union was where I pushed a shopping cart laden with groceries to feed a family of five. Grand Union, where countless times I said, "No"…"Yes"…Later"…"I don't have enough money"…"Not enough time"…Next time."

Grand Union was also where, as time passed, only a few groceries would roll around the bottom of my nearly empty shopping cart, a clanking testament to another crumbled, broken marriage in suburbia.

Grand Union: After nearly 50 years on the Post Road, the signs plastered in the windows just before the store's closing read: "All Sales Final." "Thirty Percent Discount." "Clearance," "This Store is Closing."

I made a calculated effort to get to the store on the day it was to close. Mentally, I had a long list of things I wanted to do just one more time.

I began in the produce department, remembering how my Armenian mother-in-law had taught me how to pick out the green peppers and the zucchini for making Dolma. The recipe was actually quite simple: a mixture of chopped meat, raw rice and parsley blended with just the right amount of tomato sauce to stuff the vegetables. The key was in selecting firm vegetables and in scooping out the zucchini without cutting into the skin.

My mother-in-law would love to visit Fairfield, Connecticut, in the summer, a chance to get away from her house in Bayside, Queens, New York. She would enjoy the visits with her son and grandchildren, walking along Fairfield Beach, remembering another time, a long time ago, when she was a child looking out to the Mediterranean Sea.

I pushed the shopping cart toward the meat cases, which already were empty. Gone were the chickens, gone were the shish-kebabs, always my family's favorite for summertime barbecues. Skewered with tomatoes, green peppers, mushrooms and tomatoes, the meat was always the topic of conversation when the couples' Gourmet Club would come for Saturday night dinners. "How did you marinate this meat?" my friends would ask, as if there were a special recipe rather than Grandma's tried and true methods of just adding salt and pepper and chopped onions to a bowl of cubed lamb, which is then marinated overnight in the refrigerator.

I continued my sentimental journey, heading down the aisle of cake mixes. Where were the Betty Crocker Cherry Supreme cake mix and icing and the confetti sprinkles? That was the flavor of choice for the girls' birthdays, especially my oldest daughter, Maria.

Oh, here's the cat food aisle. Canned food or dry? How about a blend with all the necessary vitamins? Four cats - just how did we become a family with four cats? The first came from the Aspetuck Apple Barn when I was reporting in Easton, Connecticut. Matilda, the cat, needed a new home. There I was with camera slung over my shoulder, reporter's notebook in one hand and cat in the other. Matilda then had babies, and we acquired others through various kinds of adoption.

I walked down the pasta aisle. My favorite. I could never go down this aisle without thinking of my mother. Her parents were born in Italy, as were my father's parents and many of my aunts and uncles. Boxes of pasta and cans of tomatoes: crushed tomato, whole tomato, tomato paste, and tomato sauce. I had become such an authority on buying the cans and boxes. I remember standing in Grand Union one day as a young woman, just engaged, stood looking perplexed at the shelves. She turned to me and told me she was making sauce for the first time and it was for her future mother-in-law. I slipped into action explaining the difference between crushed and whole and paste and sauce.

I remember, on occasion, meeting my mother in the Grand Union. My mother, who had moved to Fairfield from Long Island soon after I moved to Connecticut, to be nearer her grandchildren, would break out in the broadest grin when, by chance, we would meet at the market. By then, I was balancing work and motherhood and saw her less and less frequently, so those brief, chance meetings in the store were even more enjoyable.

Grand Union, over the years, was a barometer of my life. When my husband and I first moved to Fairfield in 1971 with our three young children, Grand Union was like a second home. As a part-time working mother, I did my weekly shopping there, plus quick runs for bread, milk or coffee.

The biggest change in my shopping habits came after my divorce, nine years later. The size of the jars that I pulled off the shelves became smaller. As the children grew up and left for college, the jars became smaller and smaller. Soon, I was pushing the shopping cart filled with cat food, magazines and the National Enquirer. Yes, even after dear Matilda passed, I am still buying cat food, this time for Creedence, a cat I inherited from my daughter Ellen when she left home to go to college.

Creedence and I live alone in a barn on Greenfield Hill, just the two of us. He curls up near my computer when I'm writing. He climbs on my lap when I'm talking on the telephone to friends and my kids. Creedence seems to purr loudest when I'm talking to Ellen.

On Grand Union's final day, I pushed the shopping cart up and down the store aisles. Despite the bargains for 30-percent off, I couldn't get myself to take anything from the shelves.

My shopping cart may have been empty, but my heart was full.

# About the Author

Rita Papazian is a former journalist and educator with over thirty years experience writing news and feature articles that were published in a variety of publications, including "The New York Times." In recent years, she has focused on memoir writing. She is the author of "Remembering Fairfield, Connecticut: Famous People & Historic Places," "Gioacchino: Memoir of an Italian Immigrant," and "Fairfield, Connecticut: 350 Years." She has a BA and MS from Hofstra University and now lives in New Jersey.

40762835R00129

Made in the USA
Columbia, SC
17 December 2018